The Amazing Story

of

Pakistan's Christians

A look back over 2,000 years of Christian history
in the land we now know as Pakistan

compiled by

Michael Wakely

British Library Cataloguing in Publication Data
A catalogue record for this book is available from the British Library.

ISBN 978-1-915046-82-6

Cover design by Angela Selfe
Art direction by Sarah Grace

Printed in the UK

Commendations

 All-Party Parliamentary Group for the Pakistani Minorities

The officers of the All-Party Parliamentary Group (APPG) for Pakistani Minorities, frequently receive requests for recommendations on books detailing the history of Pakistani Christians. We are delighted to endorse a particularly noteworthy option that not only meets this need but also provides a captivating and thorough exploration of a history often overshadowed.

Authored by Mike Wakely, *The Amazing Story of Pakistan's Christians* intricately weaves through the rich tapestry of the Christian community in Pakistan, shedding light on their challenges, triumphs, and invaluable contributions to the diverse cultural landscape of the nation.

The narrative unfolds chronologically, commencing with the advent of Christianity in the region and traversing the community's evolution across various historical epochs. Mike's rigorous research lends credibility to the narrative, offering readers a nuanced understanding of the unique challenges faced by Pakistani Christians. Skilfully navigating through complex historical events, such as the partition of India in 1947 and the subsequent formation of Pakistan, the author explores the impact of these political changes on the Christian minority.

A notable strength of *The Amazing Story of Pakistan's Christians* lies in its exploration of the cultural contributions of Pakistani Christians. From their involvement in education and social work to their contributions in the defence of the country, the book underscores the significant roles played by individuals within the Christian community in shaping the nation's cultural fabric. This emphasis on cultural richness adds depth to the narrative, challenging stereotypes and fostering a more inclusive understanding of Pakistan's diverse heritage.

In conclusion, *The Amazing Story of Pakistan's Christians* stands out as a commendable contribution to the historiography of Pakistani

Christians. Mike has adeptly illuminated a lesser-known chapter of South Asian history, offering readers a thought-provoking journey through the struggles and triumphs of a resilient community. The book serves as a testament to the author's dedication to preserving and celebrating the diverse heritage of Pakistan and is an essential read for anyone intrigued by the intersection of faith, history and cultural diversity in the country.

Morris Johns
Admin Secretary: APPG for Pakistani Minorities

(Note: Further details of the work of the APPG in the UK Parliament are given at the end of the book.)

From: **Dr Carol Walker**
Former missionary in Pakistan with Interserve and
Tutor at All Nations Christian College, UK

I have found the book an enlightening read, and wish I had had access to the opening chapters when I was first preparing to go to Pakistan. Some bits are familiar, whilst other bits were fresh, new to me, and thrilling.

From: **Dr Samuel Naaman**
Professor, Department of Intercultural Studies
Moody Bible Institute, Chicago

Brother Mike takes us on a journey through Pakistan, its history, contribution, and the legacy of Western missionaries – but not least the acknowledgement of nationals in this great legacy. Few people have taken the pain to research like Mike has, to dig deep into our history and honor both Western and nationals as they served and are still serving in my land of birth, Pakistan.

I met Mike in February 1980 when he led an OM travelling team to Sukkur in Sindh, Pakistan. In the week-long ministry, I rededicated my life, changed my major in college and joined OM. The Lord provided an opportunity to study Theology in Korea and Missiology in the US. For 25 years I have been teaching at Moody Bible Institute, Chicago, as Professor of Intercultural Studies.

Exceptional scholarly historical work by brother Mike! This book is full of stories and political events that shaped the country and Christian community of Pakistan. This is really a treasure for the Church and Mission historians and an inspiration for young Pakistani Christians to be proud of their own heritage. I consider this a "Legacy of Grace" where the contribution of Western missionaries as well as nationals is acknowledged and celebrated. During the last 40 years that I have followed brother Mike's ministry, this is a special gift to Christians worldwide. I am so grateful for this book and highly recommend it to both Christians and non-Christians.

Mike's love of Pakistan is evident in starting the charity Starfish Asia, focused on educating children from humble backgrounds in Pakistan. I highly recommend this book to all who wish to peek into the history of Pakistani Christians. I will be using material from this precious treasure in my teaching at Moody and beyond.

From: **Msgr Dr Michael Nazir-Ali**
(See his profile in Chapter 23)

Thank you for sight of this labour of love. Your even handedness with the different churches is very commendable. Your work should build confidence.

From: **Rev. Tariq Waris**
Principal Designate: Full Gospel Assemblies Bible Seminary, Lahore

Mike Wakely has done a great service to the Pakistani as well as the global church by providing us this valuable book. This work is an excellent survey of the history of Christianity in Pakistan. It is wide in scope, accessible in style, ecumenical in nature, and relevant to all in its appeal. Both clergy and laity will equally benefit from it. I wholeheartedly recommend this book to all those who are interested in the story of Christianity in Pakistan.

Contents

Foreword   7

Preface   8

Introduction: The Amazing Story
Chapter 1   9

Part 1: From Bethlehem
to the Delhi Sultanate (1526)
Chapters 2 to 4   14

Part 2: From the Mughal Empire (1526)
to the Sikh Empire (1847)
Chapters 5 to 7   29

Part 3: From the Start of Missionary Work (1849)
to the Revival in Sialkot (1900)
Chapters 8 to 12   46

Part 4: From Missionary Commitment (1850)
to the Growing Church (1900)
Chapters 13 to 16   73

Part 5: From Growing Church (1900)
to Established Church (1947)
Chapters 17 to 20   96

Part 6: From the Birth of Pakistan (1947)
to the Present Day
Chapters 21 to 30   120

Bibliography   180

Foreword

by Dr James Shera, MBE

The absence of a comprehensive book chronicling the history of Pakistani Christians has long been a matter of personal concern to me over the years. Mike Wakely has now fulfilled this crucial task.

Although originally hailing from the UK, he has devoted a considerable portion of his life to volunteer work, particularly in the realm of enhancing educational opportunities for the underprivileged Christian population in Pakistan. He has helped to uplift a whole generation of Christians by providing education to the poorest students through his charity Starfish Asia. He has justifiably earned the honorary status of being embraced as a Pakistani Christian by the local community.

My direct acquaintance with Mike may not span a significant duration, but I am well aware that the work he has dedicated himself to merits not only appreciation from Pakistanis but gratitude from people worldwide. Through his authorship of this significant book, he has delved into the past, connecting the local Christian history to its roots dating back 2,000 years, thus debunking the notion that their faith was an import brought by British colonists in the nineteenth and twentieth centuries. This contribution is a priceless gift to the Pakistani Christian community. This book offers readers the latest insights and comprehensively covers the pivotal role played by the Pakistani Christians in the history of the country.

Mike's relentless dedication to this project deserves recognition. As an outsider with deep connections to the country, he brings a unique perspective, presenting a distinctive history of Pakistani Christians. I wholeheartedly recommend this book, not only for the general reader but also as a valuable resource for future historians. It is indeed a treasure trove of knowledge and insight.

Dr James Shera, MBE, *Hilal-e-Quaid Azam, Sitara-e-Pakistan*
(See his profile in Chapter 23)

Preface

This book was first prepared as a textbook for Pakistan's Christian students. As far as we can tell, no such attempt has been made to survey the history of Christianity in the area that is today known as Pakistan – with the exception of an excellent study course produced by the Open Theological Seminary in Lahore. Today's Christians in Pakistan need to know more about their rich history that stretches back for 2,000 years – and we feel the world needs to hear the story too! The project was conceived and planned for Pakistan's Christians, but we think you will also enjoy the journey.

This is not an academic or comprehensive survey. It is a story – actually many stories of events, people and personalities – designed to be an enjoyable and inspiring read.

I am not a Pakistani though I have lived in and loved Pakistan, and given much of my life to the welfare of Pakistan's Christian minority. I owe credit to a number of Pakistani Christians who have inspired me to compile this story and have helped to correct and advise me.

Firstly, I have had numerous helpful discussions with Asif Aqeel, a writer and researcher living in Lahore. I had hoped he would write the book, but he is busy with many other projects. I also owe much credit to David Diwan, a Christian publisher in Lahore, who urged me to keep going and who has published it in Urdu and English for students. I have greatly valued advice from Ms Freda Carey who, together with the Rev. Majeed Abel, wrote the Christian History course for the Open Theological Seminary. Rev. Tariq Waris, a wise and capable friend and Vice-Principal of the Full Gospel Assemblies Bible Seminary in Lahore, has been a positive and encouraging influence. I am also very thankful to Msgr Dr Michael Nazir-Ali, who has sent much encouragement together with invaluable advice.

And of course special thanks to my wife, Kerstin, who thinks the stories in the book are fascinating. I agree.

Mike Wakely
November 2023

Chapter 1

Introduction: The Amazing Story

Pakistan is often a much misunderstood land, better known for its extremist violence, economic and political turmoil or the tragic abuse and persecution of Christians and other minorities.

This book isn't about all that. Our story is full of good news about an amazing community with an astonishing and rich history: the amazing history of Pakistan's Christians.

Who are Pakistan's Christians?

Surely Pakistan is a Muslim country. Surely Christians are a tiny minority and have little freedom to meet or worship. Surely Pakistan is high on the list of countries where Christians are persecuted and there is little religious freedom. Surely you have heard all this before…

Surely… surely… in fact there are three to four million Christians in Pakistan today, and their Constitution gives them full freedom to practise and propagate their faith. That is not the story we often hear.

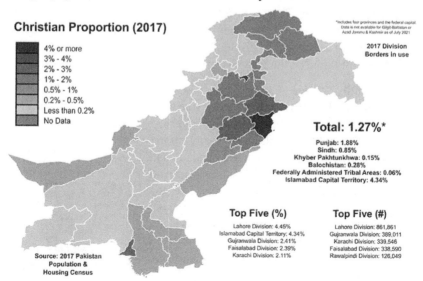

Christian Proportion (2017)

- 4% or more
- 3% - 4%
- 2% - 3%
- 1% - 2%
- 0.5% - 1%
- 0.2% - 0.5%
- Less than 0.2%
- No Data

*Includes four provinces and the federal capital. Data is not available for Gilgit-Baltistan or Azad Jammu & Kashmir as of July 2021

2017 Division Borders in use

Total: 1.27%*

Punjab: 1.88%
Sindh: 0.85%
Khyber Pakhtunkhwa: 0.15%
Balochistan: 0.28%
Federally Administered Tribal Areas: 0.06%
Islamabad Capital Territory: 4.34%

Top Five (%)

Lahore Division: 4.45%
Islamabad Capital Territory: 4.34%
Gujranwala Division: 2.41%
Faisalabad Division: 2.39%
Karachi Division: 2.11%

Top Five (#)

Lahore Division: 861,861
Gujranwala Division: 389,011
Karachi Division: 339,546
Faisalabad Division: 338,590
Rawalpindi Division: 126,049

Source: 2017 Pakistan Population & Housing Census

Pakistan has only existed as a nation since 1947. Before that date, the land area was part of India. It has gone through many identities over the past 2,000 years, as you will read in this history. But essentially the area has been populated for many centuries by people speaking Punjabi (in Punjab), Sindhi (in Sindh), Baluchi (in Baluchistan) and Pashtu (in the North-West Frontier, now known as Khyber Pakhtunkhwa). These are the major areas of modern Pakistan, but prior to 1947 they were all part of India.

The majority people have been successively Zoroastrian, Buddhist, Hindu, Sikh and now Islamic. And in the midst of all that turmoil there have been Christians – at times very few and over the last 200 years an increasing and significant number. Today, the Government statistics say there are about 3 million, though many believe the figure is much higher.

Why do we need to write their history?

There are several reasons for looking back and telling the story of Pakistan's Christians.

1. The first is that it is an amazing and great story. It began a long time ago, though the early part is called a legend, and the story may have been embroidered in the telling. But it is possible that there was a Wise Man from Punjab in Bethlehem when Jesus was born – and there were possibly Jews from Punjab in Jerusalem on the Day of Pentecost. Evidence is strong that the Apostle Thomas spent a lot of time in Punjab in the first century. Read on… it is a great story.

2. Secondly, some extraordinary and heroic missionaries have committed their lives to work in this area. The Jesuits who tried to convert the great Mughal Emperor Akbar – the pioneers who opened schools and hospitals, and many more. Their dedication, perseverance and sacrifice needs to be told and known. And then the tale of Punjabi saints like the sadhu, Sundar Singh, who disappeared into Tibet, and the converts from Sikhism, Hinduism and Islam. Today we can learn much from their dedication, leadership and example.

3. Thirdly, this book was written to encourage and inspire Pakistan's own Christian communities. It was conceived to open the eyes of Pakistani high school students as part of their Christian curriculum. Pakistani Christians have much to be proud of. They have an amazing heritage in a long line of gifted Christian politicians, teachers, doctors and pioneers who have served with devotion and courage to improve the lives of Pakistani citizens, and to bring the Gospel of Christ to those who are hungry for God, and especially the downtrodden and the poor.

4. It is a story to be celebrated. It deserves to be more widely known. Today we build on yesterday's foundations. Pakistan's Christians today need to know the foundations of their community in order to stand against the storms that tomorrow might bring. When they know who they are and where they come from, then maybe they can dream how they can change the world and make it a better place for those who live after them.

5. And finally, this is a story that tells how much God cares for the peoples of every age. A large part of the Bible is history. It tells us what happened in the past and how God has been active throughout all the centuries. History is truly the story of God, His world and His people. We need to know that story better.

Where our story begins

The story of Pakistan's Christians really begins in the Garden of Eden with Adam and Eve. We are all the descendants of Adam and Eve. The historical record in Genesis tells us that they sinned and rebelled against God. It was the beginning of many of our problems.

God punished those sinful people by sending a great flood. Read about it in Genesis chapters 5 to 7. Noah was saved, together with his family and thousands of animals. After the flood, the Bible tells us that Noah's three sons left Mount Ararat (in today's eastern Turkey) and travelled in different directions.

Many ancient traditions tell that the descendants of Noah's son Shem travelled east towards Persia and then on into India. It is possible that they helped to found the Indus civilisation, including the great archaeological sites in Pakistan, Mohenjodaro and Harappa in southern Punjab. We cannot be certain, but it is likely that the Punjabi people are descended from the sons of Shem.

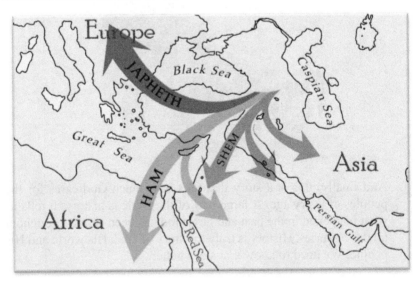

Mohenjodaro

Mohenjodaro ("the Mound of the Dead") is a ruined city, built entirely of unbaked brick, in southern Pakistan. Built about 2,300 years before Christ, it was the largest settlement of the ancient Indus Valley Civilisation, about 3 miles in circumference. It was one of the world's earliest major cities, contemporaneous with the civilisations of ancient Egypt, Mesopotamia and Minoan Crete. With an estimated population of at least 40,000 people, Mohenjodaro prospered until around 1700 BC.

Sometime between 1800 and 1500 BC (Before Christ) a large tribe, known as Aryans, meaning "noble people" in the Sanskrit language, came from central Asia and invaded the Indian subcontinent. They brought with them specific religious traditions. Most history of this period is derived from the Vedas, the oldest scriptures in the Hindu religion, which were composed by the Aryans in Sanskrit. This was about the same time that the Israelites were led out of Egypt by Moses.

The Aryans conquered the inhabitants of the Indus Valley Empire and made them into their servants and slaves. These peoples became the outcastes of the Aryan Hindu caste system. Many of Pakistan's Christians today are the descendants of these original inhabitants of the five rivers of Punjab.

Part 1

(Chapters 2 to 4)

From Bethlehem to the Delhi Sultanate (1526)

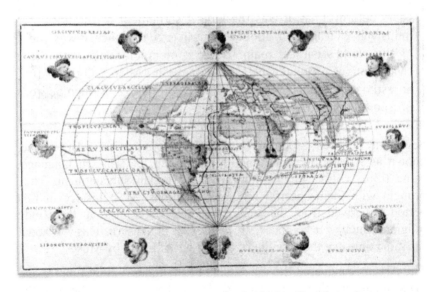

This is a world map drawn in Italy by Battista Agnese in 1544.

Chapter 2

Punjabis in the New Testament

Was one of the Wise Men a Punjabi?

It may be a surprise to discover that Pakistan's Christian history possibly began in about 4 BC when the Wise Men (or *Magi*) travelled *"from the east"* to Bethlehem.

"After Jesus was born in Bethlehem in Judea, during the time of King Herod, Magi from the east came to Jerusalem and asked, 'Where is the one who has been born king of the Jews? We saw his star when it rose and have come to worship him.'" (Matthew 2:1-2)

Who were these *"Magi from the east"*? The word Magi means "scholars and priests" or Wise Men. They followed a star and were therefore probably astrologers, looking to the heavens to guide them. They followed a significant sign which told them that a King was to be born near Jerusalem. They travelled for many months and many miles to see the Child and to worship Him.

Their journey brought them *"from the rising of the sun"*. It is very probable that they came from the Persian Empire – known at that time as Parthia, which stretched from eastern Syria to the fringes of India. There is a very old Armenian tradition that the *"Magi of Bethlehem"* were named Balthasar from Arabia, Melchior from Persia, and Casper (sometimes also known as Gaspar, Kaspar or Jasper) from India.

In 1370 a Carmelite scholar, Johannes of Hildesheim, took on an ambitious task to compile an account, titled the ***History of the Three Kings***, a collection of stories taken from various biblical, historical and legendary sources. It is possible that he just made up a fictitious account – but it is perhaps more likely that Johannes of Hildesheim had access to stories passed on from one generation to another, legends and sources no longer available to us that pointed back to real history.

Johannes of Hildersheim wrote that they each learned of the star over Bethlehem and journeyed from their respective lands – and one of them, Casper, passed through the city of Taxila (now in Pakistan) on his way to Bethlehem.

He continued his tale, that from Bethlehem the three men returned to India, where many years later they met the Apostle Thomas, who consecrated them as bishops. It may not be true, but it is intriguing to think that there is a possible connection between Taxila and the Wise Men who worshipped the baby Jesus. Casper may indeed have been a Punjabi.

Johannes of Hildersheim continued his story, recounting that the three kings (now bishops) died and their remains were ultimately taken to Milan in Italy and thence to Cologne, where they lie still in the cathedral. Johannes died in 1375, but his book lived on.

After Pentecost: *"Go into all the world!"*

After His death and resurrection, Jesus had called His disciples to meet Him on the Mount of Olives near Jerusalem.

There, just before He returned to heaven, He gave His final instructions to the disciples. Among them was Thomas, the doubter, now convinced that Jesus had risen from the dead. The future of the church was in their hands.

"Go and make disciples of all nations, baptising them in the name of the Father and of the Son and of the Holy Spirit...
you will be my witnesses in Jerusalem, and in all Judea and Samaria, and to the ends of the earth."

(Matthew 28:19, Acts 1:8)

Among the crowds on the Day of Pentecost

The Book of Acts tells us what happened after Jesus left them. Before He was taken up, He told the disciples: *"Stay in the city until you have been clothed with power from on high"* (Luke 24:49). So they waited together in the Upper Room – 120 disciples, unsure what was going to happen next. It was the time of Pentecost – a Jewish festival held every year 50 days after the Passover. The Jews came together to Jerusalem  in large numbers to celebrate the giving of the Ten Commandments to Moses at Mount Sinai.

That is why, on the Feast Day of Pentecost, *"there were staying in Jerusalem God-fearing Jews from every nation under heaven"* (Acts 2:5). And that is the day that the Holy Spirit fell on the disciples with the sound of a mighty wind and tongues of fire hovering over their heads.

Where had all these Jewish worshippers come from? Luke tells us:

"Parthians, Medes and Elamites; residents of Mesopotamia, Judea and Cappadocia, Pontus and Asia, Phrygia and Pamphylia, Egypt and the parts of Libya near Cyrene; visitors from Rome (both Jews and converts to Judaism); Cretans and Arabs." (Acts 2:9-11)

They came from many countries, but among them were Parthians. Who were the Parthians? Where had they come from? Parthia was the land of Persia, a huge empire that stretched all the way to the Indus River – modern Pakistan. It is possible that some ancestors of Pakistan's Christians today were in that crowd on the Day of Pentecost.

Historian and bishop S. K. Das believes there was a Jewish community in Taxila in the first century, which would strengthen this supposition. Maybe some of them took the Gospel back to the Indus River in Punjab – maybe preparing for the Apostle Thomas to arrive in Taxila a few years later.

Chapter 3

The Apostle Thomas in Taxila

After Pentecost: into all the world

The disciples returned to Jerusalem, as Jesus told them, and there they waited until the Holy Spirit fell on them. After Pentecost the believers were scattered to many places, partly due to persecution and partly because they were eager to pass on the Good News. They began to obey the Great Commandment and to share the Gospel with both Jews and ultimately also Gentiles in their own country and beyond. The Book of Acts tells us how the Apostle Paul took the Gospel to many lands that were part of the Roman Empire, until he finally arrived in Rome.

Where did the 12 apostles go after Pentecost?

The Bible does not tell us what the other disciples did after Pentecost. But there are many stories and traditions, which may be true. This we do know: the Gospel was taken far and wide by the apostles and many other Christians who went from place to place telling people about Jesus.

- Old traditions tell us that **Simon Peter** travelled to Asia Minor, together with his wife, preaching the Gospel as they went. He was arrested, imprisoned and finally arrived in Rome. He was executed by crucifixion after about 30 years of ministry.

- **Andrew** may have travelled to the Black Sea, then to Asia Minor and finally back to Greece where he was martyred in AD 69.

- **James and John** were also missionaries. An early tradition says that James may have gone to preach the Gospel in Spain (he is known as the patron saint of Galicia), but then returned to Jerusalem where he was martyred in AD 43 (Acts 12:1).

  John visited Rome, where he was almost killed. He was then put in prison on the island of Patmos, and then went to Ephesus (in modern Greece) where he died in old age.

The Acts of Thomas

There are many ancient traditions about all the apostles. One thing is very clear – they all became church leaders, teachers and preachers, evangelists and missionaries.

However, it was the Apostle **Thomas** who seems to have travelled most widely from Jerusalem. In the fourth Gospel written by John, Thomas is also known as Didymus – both names meaning "the Twin" in Hebrew and Greek. In the Acts of Thomas he is also called Judas Thomas. Among the many legends and traditions from those early years are the stories of his travels and ministry through Parthia and on to Taxila and to South India.

Eusebius, the church historian writing in the fourth century, recorded that *"Parthia was allotted to Thomas"* as the disciples set out to take the Gospel to the world.

Perhaps the most important collections of stories was written in the third century. It is called the *Acts of Thomas*, and was written in Edessa (in modern Turkey), a city that became a centre of early Christianity. It tells how Thomas was called to be a missionary to India – and especially to the Kingdom of Gondophares located in the area of Taxila and Mardan, both now in the north of modern Pakistan.

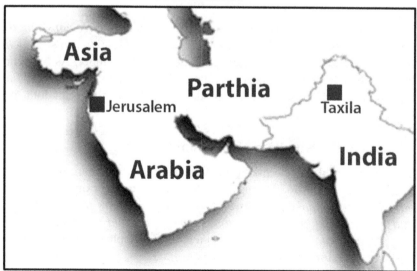

The Apostle Thomas called to preach in India

Thomas was the disciple of Jesus who doubted the resurrection. When the other disciples told him they had seen Jesus, Thomas replied: *"Unless I see the nail marks in his hands and put my finger where the nails were, and put my hand into his side, I will not believe"* (John 20:25). One week later, when Jesus showed him the nail marks in His hands, he cried out: *"My Lord and my God!"* (John 20:28).

There are several traditions that affirm that Thomas travelled to Taxila and then on to South India. One of the strongest evidences is the Mar Thoma Church in South India that claims to have been founded by the Apostle Thomas. *The Acts of Thomas* was written at least 200 years after the events they describe. The author collected the stories from others with long memories. *The Acts of Thomas* begins like this:

"At that season all we the apostles were at Jerusalem: and we divided the regions of the world, that every one of us should go unto the region that fell to him and unto the nation whereunto the Lord sent him. According to the lot, therefore, India fell unto Judas Thomas, which is also the twin..."

Thomas did not want to be a missionary. He replied: *"I have not strength enough for this, because I am weak. And I am a Hebrew: how can I teach the Indians?"* However, he prayed and he set out for India. As he went he preached to the Parthians (Persians) and Afghans, and arrived in Sirkap, a town very close to modern Taxila in the Kingdom of Gondophares.

Thomas in the Kingdom of Gondophares

The story is told that he met a businessman called Habban, who asked him what he could do. Thomas said he was a carpenter and mason. *"I have learned to make ploughs and ox-goads, and oars for ferry-boats, and masts for ships; and in stone, tombstones and monuments, and temples, and palaces for kings."* Then King Gondophares invited him to build a palace for him in Taxila.

Taxila and the Kingdom of Gondophares

Gondophares came from Parthia to found the Indo-Parthian Kingdom in the first century. He was a Zoroastrian, a religion from Persia. Very little is known about him, but many coins have been found in recent years in Afghanistan and Mardan (now in northern Pakistan) that have his name and face on them. They can be seen today in the museum in Peshawar. The Empire of Gondophares covered the area of modern Afghanistan and Pakistan.

Gondophares was not satisfied with Thomas's work, as he had given all the money to the poor. The palace was not built, and Thomas told him that it would only be finished in heaven. Gondophares was very angry with him and threw him into prison. Thomas was not discouraged: *"Fear not, but only believe, and you shall receive everlasting life in the world to come,"* he said.

We do not know if all this is exactly true, but there is strong evidence that Thomas came to Taxila to preach the Gospel during the reign of King Gondophares.

The famous Taxila Cross was found by a farmer tilling a field outside the ruins of Sirkap, close to Taxila, in 1935. It is taken as further evidence that there was a Christian community in Taxila in the first century, founded by the Apostle Thomas.

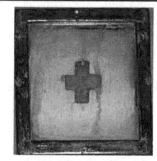

The Taxila Cross can be seen today in the Cathedral Church of the Resurrection, Lahore.

Chapter 4

Christians in Punjab for 1,000 Years

The Kingdom of Gondophares: AD 20–51

According to legend, King Gondophares threw the Apostle Thomas into prison in Sirkap and threatened to execute him. Thomas was ready to die. But then the king's brother fell seriously ill and had a vision of heaven. There he saw the palace that Thomas had promised to build for king Gondophares. Thomas was forgiven and the king converted to Christianity.

Thomas continued to preach and bring people to Christ and so the first Punjabi church was established. Sadly, King Gondophares died around AD 50, but by this time there were many new converts to the Christian faith through the preaching of the Apostle.

Thomas left the Punjab after Gondophares' death, going to Sindh and western India. He finally came to South India, where he preached the Gospel and 3,000 Hindus were converted. This infuriated the priests of the Hindu god Kali. According to Syrian Christian tradition, Thomas was killed with a spear at St Thomas Mount in Chennai on 3rd July AD 72, and his body was interred in Mylapore.

The Kushan Empire (Buddhism): AD 51–220

The Kushans were the next invaders, coming from north-west China along the Silk Route into Kashmir, Kabul and Punjab. They were traders and soldiers and they followed  the Buddhist religion. They took control of Punjab and formed an empire from AD 51 to 220. Their capital city was Peshawar.

The Kushan Buddhists were hostile towards the small Christian community, so that many moved away to Parthia (Persia) where there were by now many Christian churches. A small remnant of Christian converts remained living alongside the Buddhist Kushans.

In the next 200 years four great empires ruled the area that today stretches from England to China: the Roman Empire, Parthian (Persian), Kushan and Han Chinese.

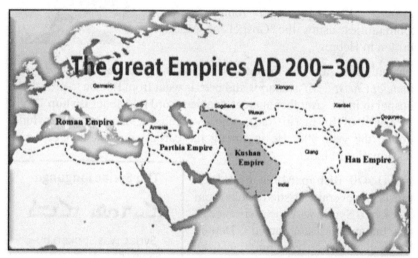

The Gupta Empire (Hinduism): AD 220–550

The Kushan Empire lasted about 200 years, and it spread the teaching of Buddhism. But great empires come and go. In the third century another warrior, Gupta, founded the **Gupta Empire** and spread the teachings of Hinduism across much of India.

It is unclear how many Christians or churches there were after the Apostle Thomas's mission. However, in the following years several Christian missionaries came to India to preach the Gospel to the Buddhists and Hindus. No doubt there were small communities of Christians in Punjab and elsewhere in India.

Christians in India in the first millennium

Eusebius, a bishop from Greece, wrote the story of the church in the fourth century, *The History of the Church*. He wrote that a philosopher called **Pantaenus** from Egypt visited India in AD 189 *"to preach Christ to the people of the East... where he found many evangelists of the Word..."* Pantaenus also found Christian communities using the Gospel of Matthew written in Hebrew.

Eusebius also said that the city of Edessa in Syria was *"devoted to the name of Christ"*. Missionaries and priests went from Edessa to preach the Gospel in India. Another ancient Arabic record told about **Bishop David** (or Dudi) of Basra (in Iraq), who evangelised many people in India around the year 300. He is among the earliest documented Christian missionaries in India.

In AD 470 **Bishop Mana** of Edessa translated several Christian books from Greek into Syriac with the assistance of an Indian priest named Daniel. Assyrian Christian communities from Persia came to India in the fourth and eighth centuries.

In the sixth century (about AD 525) a Christian sailor called **Cosmas** visited India and reported: *"There are countless churches with their own bishops and there are also monks living a disciplined Christian life."*

From all these testimonies we know that there were Christians, many in South India but also in Punjab, who acknowledged Saint Thomas as the founder of their church.

> ### The Syriac language
>
> ܠܫܢܐ ܣܘܪܝܝܐ
>
> Syriac was spoken by many Christians in the churches in Syria and Turkey in the first and second century. It is very similar to the Aramaic language spoken by Jesus.
>
> ### Edessa
>
> Edessa is an ancient city, now in Turkey, close to the border of Syria. It was a centre of great Christian learning and study in the fourth century.

The arrival of Islam in India

Muslims did not come to India as missionaries preaching peace, but as soldiers bringing conquest and destruction. Beginning in the eighth century, there were three main invasions in which Islamic armies took control of almost all India. They all arrived from Arabia and central Asia through Sindh and Punjab.

1. Muhammad bin Qasim

Muhammad bin Qasim was a young Arab military commander from close to Mecca. He set out from Arabia in AD 712 to conquer Sindh with a huge army of about 6,000 soldiers. Another 6,000 soldiers on camels arrived by sea, so it was a powerful army that marched north through Sindh.

There was little resistance from the Hindu tribes and the Muslim army conquered town after town as far north as Multan. It is said that *"he had every man over the age of 17 killed"*. He established Islamic Sharia law, but allowed the Hindus and Christians to practise their religion. He also forced them to pay the *jizya* tax to the Muslim rulers.

2. The Ghaznavid Empire, the Delhi Sultanate and the Ghurid Empire (Islam)

Mahmood Ghaznavi was born in AD 971 in Ghazni (a town in southern Afghanistan). He was a powerful military leader. In AD 998 he led a great army into Punjab and captured Multan and Lahore. Punjab became a part of the **Ghaznavid Empire** in 1021, with provincial headquarters at Lahore. Though himself a devout Muslim, he did not force Hindus to convert as a condition of service in his army.

Mahmood Ghaznavi died in 1030 and other Sultans ruled, until a greater commander, Mu'izz al-Dīn Muḥammad ibn Sām, conquered Lahore in 1186 and continued to invade India. The new empire, known as the **Ghurid Empire**, ultimately ruled most of India, including Punjab and Sindh, and established the **Delhi Sultanate**. This lasted for 300 years, with many rulers, conquests and battles.

3. The Mughal Empire

The Mughals came from many tribes in central Asia. They came through Afghanistan, Punjab and Kashmir in the thirteenth century, and were constantly at war with the Delhi Sultanate. Finally, the Mongol leader Babur conquered Delhi in AD 1526. He was a descendant of the great Mongol warriors, Timur and Genghis Khan. Babur made his headquarters in Delhi after the battle of Panipat in 1526. He founded the **Mughal Empire**.

A thousand years of Christian history in Punjab

The Apostle Thomas brought the Gospel to Punjab in the first century, about 25 years after Jesus was crucified. Christian communities lived in Punjab for 650 years before Muhammad bin Qasim brought Islam to Multan. Under his rule, Christians became a servant people and were forced to pay the Muslim *jizya* tax for *dhimmis* (non-Muslims). Many could not afford this and left for Persia or elsewhere.

From AD 1000 until Christian missionaries arrived in the court of the Mughal Emperor Akbar, there were probably very few followers of Christ in Punjab or Sindh. However, a Chinese monk called Bar Sauma, coming from China, close to the border of Baltistan, travelled to Rome in AD 1287 and told the Pope that his ancestors had been converted to Christianity by the Apostle Thomas.

The cross of Kovardo

In June 2020 an amazing discovery was made in the mountains near Skardu in northern Pakistan. A team from the University of Baltistan found an ancient Christian cross and signs that there had been Christians in Skardu more than 1,000 years ago.

The huge cross, made of marble, weighs about 4 tons, and is six metres long; it was found two kilometres from the base camps, in the mountains around the Kavardo village of Skardu in the Baltistan division, overlooking the Indus River. It is the first ever discovery, in Baltistan, of such a find, which marks the association of this land with Christianity.

Father Gulshan Barkat wrote in *DAWN* newspaper in July 2020: *"Was there a church built on the mountain and this discovery belongs to it? Was there a Christian cemetery and this cross belongs to it? Was there a monastery in Kavardo valley? Is this cross from that monastery looking down Kavardo village?"*

Another person came to see the cross in 2021. He wrote: *"During our visit to the cross of Kovardo we were surprised to see other symbols of Christian faith in the mountains, especially the symbols of a cross and a lamb. Many other symbols engraved on the mountains and hills."*

From Pentecost to 1526 : An overview

From ancient times until 1947, the modern nation of Pakistan was part of India. Our story focuses on that part of India that is now called Pakistan: Punjab, Sindh and the Frontier Provinces.

Date	Rulers and Empires	Christians
AD 30	Jerusalem was part of the Roman Empire. The Parthian Empire (Persia) ruled to the east up to the Indus River.	Parthians came to Jerusalem to celebrate Pentecost.
AD 19–50	The Kingdom of Gondophares in Sirkap. Gondophares was a ZOROASTRIAN, a Persian religion.	St Thomas in Gondophares' Kingdom.
AD 51–220	The Kushan Empire: BUDDHISM They were led by Kujula Kadphises from China. They ruled across Afghanistan and Punjab.	The Kushans persecuted the Christian community.
AD 220–550	The Gupta Empire: HINDUISM Founded by Maharaja Gupta, who spread the teachings of Hinduism.	Small Christian communities in Punjab.
AD 712–977	Muhammad bin Qasim conquered Sindh and established ISLAM.	Christians paid the *jizya* tax.
AD 977–1186	The Ghaznavid Empire: ISLAM Mahmood Ghaznavi conquered Lahore and Multan.	Limited religious tolerance.
AD 1206–1526	The Ghurid Empire and the Delhi Sultanate conquered India.	Few Christians in Punjab.
1526	The Mughal Empire: ISLAM Babur conquered Delhi.	A dark period for Christians.

Part 2

(Chapters 5 to 7)

From
the Mughal Empire (1526)
to
the Sikh Empire (1847)

Abu'l-Fazl, one of the disciples of Din-i-Ilahi, meeting the Mughal Emperor Akbar

Chapter 5

Christians and the Mughal Emperors

Babur: the first great Mughal Emperor

Babur, which means "Tiger" in Persian, was born in central Asia in 1483. He was a descendant of the Mongol ruler Genghis Khan, and he wanted to fight and conquer. After losing several battles in central Asia, he finally conquered Kabul in 1504 at the age of 21. Then he looked east, invaded Sialkot and Lahore and decided to attack and conquer the Delhi Sultanate.

Sultan Ibrāhīm Lodī was the ruler of Delhi, and Babur's armies met him at the famous battle of Panipat, 50 miles north of Delhi, on 21st April 1526. Babur had an army of 12,000 men. He occupied Delhi three days later and proclaimed himself the first Emperor of the Mughal Empire. He died four years later.

The Mughal Emperor Akbar

After the death of Emperor Babur, his son Humayun took the Mughal throne. He also fought many battles, was not always successful, and finally died in 1556. His son was called Abū al-Fath Jalāl al-Dīn Muḥammad Akbar – otherwise well known as one of the greatest Mughal emperors, Akbar the Great.

He is especially interesting for us. Though he was a Muslim, he was also very interested and open to studying other religions. He cancelled the Islamic *jizya* tax for non-Muslims, appointed Hindus to his court, and invited Christian missionaries to visit him.

The Mughal Emperor Akbar and the missionaries

The Jesuits were committed to mission – to preach the Gospel around the world. They sent missionaries to Japan and also to Goa on the west coast of India. In 1579 the Jesuit brothers in Goa received this letter from Emperor Akbar:

> *"Send me two learned priests who should bring with them the chief books of the Law and the Gospel, for I wish to study and learn the Law and what is best and most perfect in it."*

Three Jesuits (Italian, Spanish and Persian), Fathers Rudolf Acquaviva, Anthony Monserrate and Francis Henrique reached Fatehpur Sikhri near Agra on 18th February 1580. Akbar welcomed the missionaries and questioned them at length. He was presented with a new Bible in Hebrew and Greek (which he could therefore not understand), which was placed in a gold casket in his private room. *"The courtiers spent the first day questioning the authenticity of the Bible, followed by sessions about Paradise. For four days the debate continued."*

The Jesuits

The Society of Jesus, also known as the Jesuits, is a religious order of the Roman Catholic Church with its headquarters in Rome. It was founded by Ignatius of Loyola and six companions in 1540. While still a student at the University of Paris, Ignatius' experience of God captivated other students. In a chapel outside Paris, Ignatius and six of his university friends professed religious vows of poverty and chastity to bind themselves together in their dedication to God and "the betterment of souls". They called themselves "friends in the Lord", and became the first Jesuits.

They received the approval of the Pope, with this purpose: *"To strive especially for the defence and propagation of the faith and for the progress of souls in Christian life and doctrine, by means of public preaching, lectures and any other ministration whatsoever of the Word of God, and further by means of retreats, the education of children and illiterate persons in Christianity."*

Emperor Akbar was quite a complicated person. He was not an orthodox Muslim, and set out to found his own religion, which he called *Dīn-i Ilāhī* (in Persian: "Divine Faith"). It was a mixture of Hindu and Muslim beliefs and he made very few converts. Akbar continued to discuss Christianity with the Jesuits for the next three years. He gave them land to build a Catholic church not far from his palace. Though they remained hopeful that he would convert to Christianity, Akbar refused to commit himself. The Jesuits returned, disappointed, to Goa in 1582.

Akbar moved his capital to Lahore in 1585. He built the famous Lahore Fort. Then suddenly a letter was received by the Jesuits in Goa in 1590, inviting them to Lahore. This was the beginning of three more missions that were to come to Lahore. They stayed at a royal house located just off Tehsil Bazaar. The aim of their mission was *"to concentrate on converting the emperor"*.

On 28th August 1595, Akbar called them to court. It is said that he ordered them to *"build a church and convert as many people as they could"*. The Jesuits were shocked. The emperor contributed 4,000 rupees towards the building of the church and a house. That church, made of wood with numerous balconies and decorated with pictures, held its first service on 7th September 1597.

After the death of Emperor Akbar

At Lahore Father Pinheiro was left in charge of the church and 38 people, mostly Hindus, became Christians. This caused some trouble for the missionaries, but the new emperor Jahangir favoured the Christians. At one time he even wore a cross around his neck and he provided 80 rupees a month for the expenses of the church in Lahore. Jahangir instructed three of his nephews to become Christians and they were baptised publicly in 1610. About 1,000 Christians lived in Lahore in 1614, many of them foreign businessmen.

Emperor Jahangir and Jesus, painted in 1610 by the Mughal artist Abu'l-Hasan

In 1614 the Jesuits bought land at Mozang for Lahore's first Christian graveyard. They were always treated as honoured guests and given a warm welcome. They continued to hope that the emperor might become a Christian.

Then suddenly Jahangir changed his mind. His nephews were returned to Islam, and the Jesuits bitterly remarked that they had *"rejected the light"*. Due to political disagreements with the Portuguese government, which was regarded as Christian, Jahangir ordered that the church be shut and the Fathers expelled from the college. This lasted a short time before he allowed the church to open again. Jahangir died of illness in October 1627.

The next emperor, Shah Jahan, had a very different attitude. He was hostile towards the Jesuit missionaries and did all he could to hinder their work. He ordered the execution of his nephew Huang who had converted to Christianity. His son, however, had a much more tolerant and even benevolent attitude towards the Christians. He counted Jesuits among his intimate friends.

The Great Mughal Emperors

The Mughal Empire lasted from 1526 until 1857. Of the 19 emperors, only six could be called "great".

❶ Babur (1526–1530)

Babur imposed a tax on Christians, but was otherwise a tolerant Muslim.

❷ Humayun (1530–1556)

Humayun was still learning how to rule in a Hindu community. As a Muslim, he accepted the rights of all religions.

❸ Akbar (1556–1605)

Akbar was married to Hindu, Muslim and Christian ladies, and was open to learn from all religions. He invited the missionaries from Goa to discuss Chrtistianity, and allowed them to build churches in Agra and Lahore.

❹ Jahangir (1605–1627)

Jehangir favoured the Christians and encouraged missionary work.

❺ Shah Jahan (1628–1628)

Shah Jahan disliked Christians, banned conversion, destroyed the churches and imprisoned the Jesuits.

❻ Aurangzeb (1628–1658)

Aurangzeb was a pious Muslim. He imposed Sharia law and demanded the *jizya* tax from minority religions. After his death the empire began to fail. Battles were fought and lost and the 12 emperors who ruled from Delhi lost power to new conquerors.

❼ Bahadur Shah II (1837–1857)

Bahadur Shah Zafar was the last Mughal emperor. He died in 1862.

Chapter 6

The Arrival of Foreigners

Events in faraway Portugal

While the Mughal emperors were taking control of all India, events far away were taking place that would affect the future. In June 1497 an explorer from Portugal, Vasco da Gama, sailed with a fleet of four vessels around Africa. Nine months later they arrived in Calicut on the south coast of India. He died in 1524, having been nominated as "the Governor of Portuguese India" and establishing a colony of Portuguese businessmen in Goa. They began to bring Indian spices to Europe.

Francis Xavier was born in 1506 in Spain. Together with Ignatius of Loyola, they founded the Society of Jesus (known as the Jesuits). In 1540 King John of Portugal requested the Jesuits to send missionaries to spread the message of Christianity to India. Francis Xavier and two other Jesuits arrived in Goa in 1542. Within a few years there was a strong Christian community in Goa.

It was from Goa that three Jesuits came to the court of Emperor Akbar in 1580, and so the Gospel came to Agra and then Lahore (Chapter 5).

Opposition and persecution

The Mughal Emperor Shah Jahan claimed the throne of the Mughal Empire after his father Jahangir died. He was a cruel and ambitious ruler, and murdered any of his family who threatened him. He killed his brother, his two cousins and his nephews – anyone he thought would be a threat to his power. He is also famous for many wonderful buildings, the most famous being the Taj Mahal in Agra.

He may have been a great ruler, but his strength lay in his ruthlessness. In 1633 he ordered all Christian places of worship to be closed. The church in Lahore was destroyed, and he issued an order making all conversion from Islam illegal. It was the end of the Jesuit mission to Punjab. There was a Catholic Mission in Thatta in Sindh until 1672 when that also closed. Many of the Christians in Lahore moved away, though there always remained some who were faithful and continued to keep the Christian faith. It was a bleak and difficult time for Christians living in Punjab.

At the same time in England

In England businessmen were watching the success of the Portuguese spice trade. Portugal was becoming rich with the trade in Indian spices – other countries wanted to trade also. So in 1600 a group of English businessmen founded a company to be known as the "East India Company". They bought a ship called the *Red Dragon*, and sailed to Indonesia. In 1608 they arrived in India and five years later established a factory at Surat in the Indian State of Gujarat. It was the beginning of England's involvement with India that finally became an empire.

The East India Company was essentially a trading company, and not a missionary society. It grew quickly, as more and more spices were exported from India to Europe.

With Emperor Jahangir's permission, they began to build small bases, or factories, across India. Initially they were just used for storage and trade. However, as the business grew, more European businessmen and staff came to India to manage the purchases and export. As they needed protection for their staff, soldiers and police also came from Europe, until by the end of the eighteenth century the East India Company had an army of 200,000 men, mostly Indians with British officers, to protect their business interests.

The World

The Jesuits came from Spain and Portugal.

The British came from England, Scotland and Ireland.

It is about 5,000 miles direct to Lahore, but they came by ship, nearly 15,000 miles.

Missionaries and Christians 1600–1800

Together with businessmen and soldiers, the East India Company sent chaplains to look after the spiritual needs of the Company. They were not missionaries, though the East India Company appointed them for *"the spreading of the Gospel in India... and to teach the people in building them up in the knowledge of God and faith in Jesus Christ"*. Their main task was to be pastors for the foreigners.

The East India Company lasted for 258 years until 1857. During these years 665 chaplains served in India. Evangelism among the Hindus and Muslims was not allowed by the Company. However, evangelistic passion was evident among the chaplains. Books and letters urged their supporters in England to pray that India would accept the Christian message. One godly chaplain was Henry Lord, who spent six years in Surat (now in Indian Gujrat, 450 miles from Karachi) between 1624 and 1630. He wrote a book that prepared the way for missionaries to come to India. The Rev. Henry Lord's vision was *"that we may pray that God would establish us in His truth; His Word is that truth"*.

At the same time in Punjab: the Sikh Empire

At the time that the great Mughal emperors were conquering most of India – and while the Europeans (especially the Portuguese and the British) were setting up their business centres around the coast of India, something different was happening in Punjab.

Sikhism was founded by Guru Nanak, born into a Hindu family in 1469 in Nankana Sahib (now in Pakistan). His followers increased in number, especially in Punjab. Emperor Akbar supported all religions and especially favoured Sikhism because of its generous ideals. The Mughals and Sikhs lived in harmony until Akbar's death in 1605.

Later Mughal emperors regarded the Sikhs as enemies. Jahangir executed Arjun Devi, a Sikh leader, and Shah Jahan attacked the Sikh centre at Amritsar, close to Lahore. The Sikhs formed an army and fought many battles against the Mughal Muslims.

> **Who are the Sikhs?**
>
> Sikh means "disciple" or "learner". Sikhism developed from the spiritual teachings of Guru Nanak (1469–1539), the faith's first guru. He formed a group of disciples who believed (unlike the Hindus) that there is one God. His teachings can be found in the Sikh scripture, the *Guru Granth Sahib,* a collection of verses recorded in Gurmukhi. Sikhism stresses the importance of doing good actions rather than merely carrying out rituals.

Maharaja Ranjit Singh, the Lion of Punjab

Ranjit Singh, born in Gujranwala in 1780, came to be known as Sher-e-Punjab ("The Lion of Punjab"). He united the Sikh forces and led them to victory. They captured Lahore in 1799 and established the Sikh Empire with its capital in Lahore. Ranjit Sigh ruled his empire for almost 40 years. He died in 1839. His tomb is a gold-covered building in Lahore, located next to the Lahore Fort and the Badshahi Mosque.

Christians in the Sikh Empire

Ranjit Singh gave the Punjab four decades of peace and prosperity. He showed equal respect to citizens of all faiths. They were allowed to freely practise their religions without payment of any special tax.

Many people from Europe, mostly French and Italian, and some from British India, came to work for the Maharaja in administration and the army. Some became influential and leading personalities at the Court of Lahore. In 1829 a Roman Catholic priest came to Lahore and stayed for two years as priest for about 50 Christians.

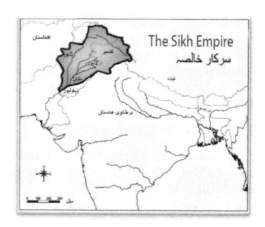

John Lowrie: first missionary to Punjab

In 1834 an American missionary, John Cameron Lowrie, arrived in India. He was the first Presbyterian missionary to India and he moved to Ludhiana in Punjab. His aim was to bring the Gospel to the Punjabis, and he believed in the value of education as a way to introduce people to the Christian faith. *"The missionary's schools are his churches,"* he said. *"The scholars his congregation, and every day is hallowed by him in giving and applying Christian knowledge."*

He took over a small English-medium school in Ludhiana. *"Some fourteen or sixteen native boys had been in attendance. After a few weeks the number was increased to about fifty."* The school consisted of Hindus, Sikhs, Christians and Muslims and grew to about 70 students.

The Rev. Lowrie was surprised when he received an invitation from Maharaja Ranjit Singh to visit Lahore. *"He had heard of me and of our English school, and with his invitation he made a proposal that I should take charge of the education of a number of the young Sikh noblemen."* The Maharaja was polite and welcomed him. Lowrie gave him a Bible, and Ranjit Singh asked him: *"Where is God?"* Lowrie replied: *"God is everywhere present; he has made known in his holy Word, how we should worship him."* They had an interesting conversation about God and faith. Ranjit Singh welcomed the opening of the school, but refused to allow Christianity to be taught. John Lowrie was not willing to start a school in Lahore if he could not teach Christianity, so he returned to Ludhiana. He stayed there for two years, active in mission service until his death in 1900.

The end of the Sikh Empire

After Ranjit Singh's death, the Sikh Empire began to fail. After two wars with the British Indian army, Punjab became part of the British Indian Empire in 1849.

Ranjit Singh's seven-year-old son, Duleep Singh, became a Maharaja. He was exiled to Britain at the age of 15 and became a friend of Queen Victoria, who wrote of him: *"Those eyes and those teeth are too beautiful."* In 1853 he converted to Christianity, but later regretted this decision and reconverted to Sikhism.

Chapter 7

The Great Bible Translators

William Carey, the father of modern missions

On 17th August 1761 a baby boy was born in a small village in the centre of England. His parents named him William – William Carey. His parents were Christians. His father was a cloth weaver and later became a teacher in the local school. Young William loved to study plants, insects and birds – and he loved books. Then he learned the art of making shoes, and he committed his life to follow Jesus Christ.

> **William Carey wrote:**
>
> *"Our Lord Jesus Christ commissioned his apostles to 'Go into all the world, and preach the gospel to every creature.' This commission was as extensive as possible, and laid them under obligation to go into every country of the habitable globe, and preach to all the inhabitants, without exception, or limitation."*

As a young man he began to preach in the local church, and he taught himself to read New Testament Greek. Then he studied Latin and Hebrew. He was a school teacher and a pastor. He was clever, he was ambitious and he always refused to give up.

Carey was also very troubled that so many people in the world had never heard the Good News of the Gospel. He wanted to become a missionary.

He was a man of vision, passion and faith. He wrote: *"Expect great things from God, receive great things from God."* In 1792, at the age of 31, together with several friends, he formed a society, later known as the Baptist Mission Society.

William Carey in India

William Carey sailed to India in April 1793 and arrived in Calcutta in November. To support himself he worked as the manager of a factory making dyes for cloth, but his great ambition was to preach the Gospel. He immediately started to study Indian languages and was very soon able to preach in Bengali.

Carey was joined by a printer, William Ward, who opened a printing shop. Joshua and Hanna Marshman opened schools for children, and Carey began teaching at Fort William College in Calcutta. In December 1800 Carey baptised his first convert, Krishna Pal, and two months later, he published his first Bengali New Testament.

Over the next 28 years, he and his co-workers translated the whole Bible into six of India's major languages and parts of the Bible into 209 other languages. Carey went through great suffering and disappointment, including a terrible fire that destroyed much of his work in 1812. He responded: *"We are cast down but not in despair."* The first Punjabi Bible was printed in 1815 in Calcutta. William Carey stayed in India for 41 years. He never visited Punjab or other parts of India and died in 1834.

The first Punjabi Bible

The Punjabi Bible, nearly complete, was printed at the Baptist Mission Press in Serampore, near Calcutta, in 1815. William Carey himself said that the Punjabi Bible had become more popular among the Sikhs of Punjab than anywhere else in India.

> *"The book of Jesus is spoken of, is read, and has caused a considerable stir in the minds of the people."*

It was said that a Thug (thief and murderer) was asked how he could have committed so many murders. He pointed to the Punjabi Bible and said, *"If I had had this book I could not have done it."*

A *fakir* (Muslim holy man), living near Ludhiana, read the book, founded a community of worshippers of the Sachi Pitè Isa (Jesus), and suffered much persecution.

Printing in 1800

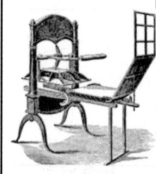

This was the kind of printing press used by William Carey at the Baptist Mission Press to print the first Punjabi Bible in 1815. Each page had to be inserted into the machine by hand. Then the lead type was covered with ink, and the handle pressed to bring the type in contact with the paper. It was a long and difficult task.

Henry Martyn and the Urdu Bible

Henry Martyn was born in 1781 in Truro in the south of England. He studied at Cambridge University and it was there that he heard a preacher tell the story of William Carey's work in India. This touched his heart and he felt that God was calling him also to go to India to preach the Gospel.

Martyn arrived in India in 1805. He began learning Hindustani (Urdu) during the nine months' long sea voyage. When he finally arrived in Calcutta, he served as a chaplain with the East India Company in Dinapore (near Calcutta), and Kanpur in central India. But his true passion was to translate the Bible into Urdu.

Within less than five years, he had translated the New Testament into Urdu and Persian and had supervised its translation into Arabic. He was not only an expert in Indian languages but also in the original languages of the Bible, Greek and Hebrew. He usually preached in Urdu and established an Urdu-speaking church in Kanpur (formerly called Cawnpore).

> *"Let me burn out for God. After all, whatever God may appoint, prayer is the great thing. Oh, that I might be a man of prayer!"*

Martyn worked hard and urgently on the Urdu, Persian and Arabic translations as if he knew he only had a short time. He became ill as a result of his exertions. In 1811 he began his journey back to England overland. In Persia, he completed his revision of the Persian translation of the Bible. He died in Tokat, Turkey, in 1812, at the age of 31.

Henry Martyn's New Testament was finally printed in Calcutta at the Baptist Mission Press in 1817 after his death.

"The New Testament of Our Lord Jesus Christ, Translated into the Hindoostanee Language from the Original Greek. By the Rev. H. Martyn, and Afterwards Carefully Revised with the Assistance of Mirza Fitrut, and Other Learned Natives."

The first complete Urdu Bible was published in 1843. Henry Martyn's Urdu New Testament still forms the basic text of the New Testament published by the Pakistan Bible Society today.

Baptist Mission Press 1815

Sheikh Salih becomes Abdul Masih

Pakistan's Christians need to remember the name of one more person, who made a vital difference to the early translation of the New Testament. His name was Sheikh Salih and he met Henry Martyn in Kanpur in 1810.

Sheikh Salih was born in Delhi in 1776 into a well-respected Muslim family. He was committed to his religion and was recognised as a scholarly teacher. In 1810 Salih was at Kanpur and he heard Martyn preach to the poor who gathered at his door on Sunday afternoons to receive money. Salih, in his own words, went *"to see the sport"*. He was struck by the message and wanted to hear more.

Martyn gave him a job to copy out his Urdu New Testament translation. Then he asked him to bind it as a book. Salih was eager to learn more. It was reported: *"On reading the Word of God, he discovered his state, and a true description of his own heart. He soon decided in favour of the Christian religion."* Salih openly declared his faith and asked for baptism. He took the name Abdul Masih. In October 1820 he was ordained as a priest, the first convert from Islam to be ordained in the church. He died on 4th March 1827, aged 51.

The Charter Act of 1813:
Christian missionaries given freedom to preach

Every ten years the East India Company had to renew its contract with the Government in London. Until 1813 they had not allowed missionaries or chaplains to preach the Gospel to Indian Muslims and Hindus. However, several leading Christians in the British Government, including William Wilberforce in a three-hour speech, urged that the law should be changed. In 1813 a new contract was written and approved. The new Charter granted permission for missionaries from the Anglican Church (Church Missionary Society) to enter British India to preach, evangelise, and open schools and hospitals. Missionaries of other denominations and nations gained permission when the Charter was reviewed in 1833. Rev. John Lowrie was one of the first to arrive in 1834.

Part 3

(Chapters 8 to 12)

From
the Start of Missionary Work (1849)
to
the Revival in Sialkot (1900)

The Mission School in Sialkot (1880)

Chapter 8

Missionaries Who Opened Schools

The great mission societies

After the East India Company finally lifted its ban on missionary activity in 1833, there came a great change across India. Suddenly in many countries, Christians realised they could send missionaries to preach the Gospel, open schools, colleges and hospitals, print and distribute Bibles – and make converts to the Christian faith. India was suddenly "open and free".

John Lowrie went back to his home in America and wrote to them:

> *"The invitation is now sent forth, 'Look unto me and be ye saved, all the ends of the earth' (Isaiah 45:22) and 'He that believeth shall be saved; he that believeth not is condemned already' (John 3:18)."*

He wrote a *Manual of Foreign Missions*. In 1838 John Lowrie became Assistant Secretary of the Board of Foreign Missions of the Presbyterian Church in the USA. Hundreds applied to join the mission.

The same was happening in other countries, as churches invited dedicated Christian men and women to join their mission societies. Many young men and women sacrificed their jobs and their lives to travel to other countries – including India – to preach the Gospel of salvation and establish churches. The Anglican Church – through the Church Missionary Society (CMS) and the Society for the Propagation of the Gospel (SPG), aided by the Ecclesiastical Department of the Government of India – the Methodists, Scottish Presbyterians and many others formed societies to support missionary work in Punjab and all India.

Charles William Forman

Charles Forman was born on 3rd March 1821 in Washington, Kentucky, USA. He started work in the family business, making and selling rope.

One Sunday evening when Charles was 15, he was at home with his family when a young pastor joined them. They talked about religion. Charles was not interested until someone said something bad about Jesus. The young pastor was very upset and hurt by this – and so was Charles. *"This young man evidently follows Christ,"* he wrote later, *"because he loves and honours him."*

It was a turning point in his life and he committed himself to follow Christ. Five years later he was baptised. *"I felt that baptism was a surrender of myself to Christ to live for him alone."*

Obeying the command to "Go"

The young Charles Forman studied for the next seven years. While he was at Princeton Theological Seminary he thought a lot about his future. Should he stay in America and become a pastor? And then he looked at the command of Jesus: *"Go into all the world and preach the Gospel to every creature."* It was clear to him. He should become a missionary, and God had called him to India.

He left America in August 1847. It was not a quick journey. Five months later he finally arrived in Calcutta where he met a famous missionary, Dr Alexander Duff, who urged him to consider the importance of education for Indian students. Before he left Calcutta he had decided that he would establish schools in which English would be the medium of instruction.

He then began his long and tiring journey across India to Agra. In those days there were no trains, no buses and no aeroplanes. As he travelled, he studied and he wrote:

"The usual way of travel was by palanquins which were carried on men's shoulders, each set of eight men carrying the conveyance six or eight miles, three or four others carrying the luggage."

He stopped in Agra, near Delhi, as there was still a war in Punjab. In 1849 the British defeated the Sikh Empire – and only then the way was open for Charles Forman to go to Lahore.

Charles Forman in Lahore: 1849

On 19th December 1849 Charles Forman, together with another American missionary, John Newton, made the important decision to open the first English-medium school in northern India. The school was under a tree and its first pupils were three Kashmiri boys. They were paid "one pie" (*one paisa*) a day to attend. Ten days later the number had increased to seven. Mr Forman taught the boys for four and a half hours a day, and Mr Newton two and a half hours.

In 1850 the school moved to a small chapel outside the city walls. The number of pupils increased to 57. Mr Guru Das Maitra, a young Bengali Christian, was employed as Principal. His salary was 50 rupees.

Punjab 1849

In 1849 in Punjab there were estimated to be 3 million people; today (2024) there are more than 120 million. The population of Lahore numbered 100,000 (now more than 10 million), all living within the city walls. Outside the walls lay the ruins of the ancient city.

One pie or paisa in 1849

The school in Rang Mahal, Lahore

By 1852 the school was too large for the small chapel, and Forman began to look for a larger building. He found the Rang Mahal ("Palace of Colours"), a large house formerly owned by the prime minister of the Mughal emperor Shah Jahan. It was located in Lahore's old city. Forman then purchased a huge amount of scientific equipment.

By 1854 the school had become famous for its amazing science laboratory and it had attracted 200 students. Along with mathematics all students had to study the Bible. The Rang Mahal School produced the very first Punjabi dictionary. The missionaries also translated a lot of European books into Hindi, Urdu and Persian.

The Rang Mahal Christian High School

Under Dr Forman's wise management the school rapidly grew. At the end of the first year, the school had 55 Hindus, 22 Muslims and three Sikh students, which included Punjabis, Kashmiris, Bengalis, Afghans and Balochis. By 1896 student numbers reached 242. The teachers were from Punjab, Bengal, Scotland and the USA.

The school became a college and the first students graduated with a BA degree in 1890. It remained as a Christian school until the Government nationalised it in 1972.

Dr Forman learned several languages including Arabic, Sanskrit, Persian, Hindi, Punjabi and Urdu. It was said of him that whenever he passed through the streets on his way to the school, crowds of boys would follow him with cries of *"Baba Forman!"* He stayed in the Punjab for 56 years – the rest of his life. He died in Lahore in August 1894 and was buried in the Gora Kabristan (Foreigners' Cemetery). He was married twice and left seven children, five of whom became missionaries.

Forman Christian College

In 1864 Dr Forman set up the Lahore Mission College at the Rang Mahal. It moved to its current location next to the Lahore Canal in 1940. The college was nationalised in 1972, but was returned to Christian control in March 2003.

Missionaries and education

The Rang Mahal Christian High School was not the first school opened by Christians in Punjab. In 1842 the Roman Catholic Church opened the St Francis School in Anarkali. Today Anarkali is a busy bazaar, but at that time it was a residential area surrounding the tomb of a lady friend of Emperor Jahangir, popularly named Anarkali (meaning "the blossom of the pomegranate"). St Francis School became one of the most famous schools in Lahore.

After 1849 when Punjab was no longer ruled by the Sikh Empire, missionaries began to open many schools. The Mission High School in Raja Bazaar, Rawalpindi, was opened in 1856 by the Presbyterian Mission. It became the Christian Higher Secondary School and was affiliated with Calcutta University. In 1893, it was given the status of a college. In 1902, the college was separated, named Gordon College and moved to its present premises near Liaqat Bagh, but the High School remained in Raja Bazaar.

After 1850 Christian missions, both Roman Catholic and Protestant, opened many schools, which provided education of a high standard for students of all faiths. Karachi Grammar School opened in 1847, Edwardes High School in Peshawar started in 1855, Mission High School (now Pennell High School) in Bannu began in 1865 (see Chapter 14).

Christian schools nationalised by the Pakistan Government

Quite unexpectedly on 15th March 1972 the Government of Pakistan, under Zulfikar Ali Bhutto, nationalised hundreds of private schools and colleges. The Government seized properties and control of education, curriculum and the appointment of staff. This was a tragic blow to the Christian community that depended on access to good education from highly qualified Christian principals and governors. In total 3,334 institutions were taken over by the Government, consisting of 1,826 schools, 155 colleges and five technical institutes. 346 Islamic seminaries were also nationalised.

Happily, in the 1980s, under Prime Minister Mohammad Khan Junejo, and later under the direction of General Pervez Musharraf and later governments, many schools and colleges were returned to the control of their former Christian governors and principals.

Chapter 9

The 1857 War of Independence

The soldiers refuse to obey

Meerut is an Indian city close to New Delhi, about 300 miles from Lahore. On 24th April 1857 the soldiers of the 3rd Bengal Light Cavalry were on parade before their officers in the Cantonment in Meerut. They were proud soldiers, mostly Muslim and some Hindus, who served under a British commander of the East India Company.

However, on 23rd April the soldiers had been ordered to use new rifles and bullets. The rumour spread among the soldiers that these cartridges were wrapped in paper greased with pig and cow fat. They needed to be bitten to be loaded and 85 of the soldiers refused to use them. The Hindus refused because they believe the cow is holy

– and the Muslims refused to eat the pig fat. At the same time, the soldiers feared that it was a plot to convert them to Christianity.

Several soldiers were arrested and sent to prison. This made people very angry and on 10th May 1857 a riot began in the streets of Meerut. It began with violence in the late afternoon. The soldiers destroyed government buildings – the jail, record room, *kachehri* (court area) and telegraph office – and went on to destroy the bungalows in which the *Feringee* (foreigners) lived. People from the surrounding villages joined in the destruction. As well as destroying buildings, they set out to kill the European and white population of Meerut, both men and women, young and old. Twenty-two British officers were killed and 34 Indians. Once the violence was over and dusk had fallen, a group of soldiers rode off towards Delhi where they arrived in the morning of 11th May.

A British Army officer went to see what was happening in the city.

"I found a thousand soldiers dancing and leaping, calling and shouting to each other and shooting their guns in all directions." Many houses and shops in Meerut were set on fire.

The Rebellion spread across India

The angry soldiers from Meerut arrived in Delhi. There the local Indian soldiers joined the Meerut men, and restored the Mughal emperor Bahadur Shah II to power. From Delhi they moved to Kanpur and Lucknow in central India. Everywhere they went, they shot and killed the British Army officers, together with their wives and children.

The news of the violence reached Peshawar and Lahore, but both cities remained calm and peaceful. Many of the Sikh soldiers refused to fight and others were disarmed. Those Indian Christians who had converted to Islam were not harmed during the Mutiny, but converts to Christianity were attacked openly. The British were seen as *Kafir* (infidels) or *Nazrani* (meaning Christian) rather than *Feringee*.

The Battle of Jhelum

A company of soldiers was sent to Rawalpindi and Jhelum to disarm the Bengal Infantry units. In Rawalpindi, all was peaceful. However, the soldiers sent to Jhelum were met by violence. There was a whole day of fighting and 35 British soldiers of the 24th Regiment of Foot and a number of loyal Indian troops were killed by mutinous soldiers. There was some trouble in Sialkot and Rawalpindi, but the rest of Punjab remained at peace.

Sir Henry Lawrence

Lawrence College in Murree is named after Sir Henry Lawrence and a road in Lahore was named Lawrence Road – changed to Cecil Chaudhry Road in 2012.

Sir Henry Lawrence was a British military officer and statesman. He was transferred from Lahore to Lucknow in central India when the Rebellion began, and he died in the siege of that city in July 1857.

Sir John Nicholson

Nicholson Road in Lahore (now Bakht Khan Road) was named after Brigadier General John Nicholson. Nicholson was dining with his friend Sir Herbert Edwardes (after whom Edwardes College was named) at Peshawar on the evening of 11th May 1857 when news reached them of the beginning of the Indian rebellion in Delhi. He went with the army to attack the Indian forces in Delhi. The city was finally captured on 21st September. Sir John Nicholson died the next day. The commander of the Indian army in Delhi was General Bakht Khan, after whom Nicholson Road was renamed.

The Rebellion in Sialkot

Two days later the regiments in Sialkot mutinied. This time there was no one to come to the rescue. The British residents left their homes in fear to reach the old Sikh fort on the hill. On the way several were murdered by the Indian soldiers. Europeans were targeted, especially certain army officers who had treated the soldiers badly. Two doctors were killed in front of their families. On 9th July prisoners were released from jail and set out to destroy the markets and other buildings.

The murder of Thomas Hunter in Sialkot

Thomas Hunter came from a village in Scotland. He was convinced that God was calling him to missionary service in India. He was sent in 1855 by the Church of Scotland as a missionary to Punjab.

He arrived in Sialkot at the beginning of 1856 and began to study Urdu. On 14th May 1857 the news reached Sialkot of the Rebellion and the murder of Christians, missionaries and Europeans. An urgent message was received by the Presbyterian missionary, Andrew Gordon:

"Please stop your preaching for a time. Especially do not allow your Indian preachers to go out. Delhi has been captured and the European population massacred."

Andrew Gordon and some other missionaries immediately left Sialkot with George Scott, an Indian evangelist, and arrived in Lahore, where they stayed in the safety of the Lahore Fort.

Thomas Hunter, his wife Jane and their baby decided to remain in Sialkot. They were sadly murdered on 9th July by a bandit named Hurmat Khan, who had been released from prison by the rioters.

Hunter Memorial Church was built in memory of their faithful service and ultimate martyrdom. The church was opened on 22nd January 1865 and attended by nine families of the Meg caste, who were settled on surrounding farmland to establish a local Christian community, called Hunterpur (now Muslim Town, Sialkot).

Thomas and Jane Hunter

Hunter Memorial Church in 1890

The War of Independence

The Rebellion in the Indian army continued for two more years until July 1859, especially in central Indian cities: Delhi, Lucknow and Kanpur (Cawnpore). At least 13,000 British and 40,000 Indian soldiers died during the revolt – and many more ordinary citizens.

The violence of the uprising led to the British Government dissolving the British East India Company and taking direct control of India. India became a part of the British Empire of which Queen Victoria was the head, ruled locally by a viceroy.

Chapter 10

Andrew Gordon and the Sialkot Mission

Andrew Gordon called by God to India

In 1856, one year before the violent events that took place in Meerut and across India, the Christian Grammar High School was established in Raja Bazar, Rawalpindi. It was a small school but it developed and grew. In 1893 it was converted into a college, and it was named Gordon College, after the American Presbyterian missionary, Andrew Gordon.

Andrew Gordon was born on 17th September 1828 in Putnam, USA. His father was a pastor of the United Presbyterian Church. In May 1853, the Presbyterian Church resolved to establish a mission in India, and elected Andrew Gordon as its missionary. It was a hard decision for Mr Gordon, and even harder for his wife. But God commanded: *"Go!"* and so he went.

Together with his wife Rebecca and his sister Elizabeth, Andrew Gordon left by ship from New York on 28th September 1854, and arrived in Calcutta more than four months later. It took so long for the journey by sea in those days. Five months and 1,700 miles later in a palanquin (cart) carried by coolies, they arrived in Sialkot, Punjab.

Andrew Gordon and the Sialkot Mission

Andrew Gordon and Rebecca had very little money and no house to live in. He wrote: *"I reached Sialkot on 8th August with $17 (34 rupees) in hand."* He had a bed made, which cost one rupee, and lived for some time in a tent. He managed to borrow 250 rupees. His early days in Sialkot were not easy. There were a few other missionaries, but no church and very few Indian Christians. As a new missionary, he had much to learn, but he started quickly to study and learn Punjabi.

After nine weeks living in a tent, the mission provided 4,000 rupees so that he could build himself a house. With great difficulty – and often being cheated by local workers – he made a home, which became the first centre of the Sialkot Mission.

God was with Andrew Gordon. As he began language study, he met two Punjabi Christians: Elisha Swift and Abdullah Athim. They were Bible teachers from another mission, and they came to Sialkot to preach. They planned to move to another city, but God kept them in Sialkot and Gordon met them. Andrew Gordon recorded: *"That night their tent was cut open by thieves and their baggage was stolen."* They not only stayed another few days, but Elisha Swift remained with Gordon and became his co-worker and enthusiastic evangelist.

Miss Elizabeth Gordon

The first single lady to be sent to India with the Presbyterian Church was Miss Elizabeth Gordon, Andrew's sister. She arrived with her brother in 1855.

She had already gained much experience as a Sunday school teacher in America, and quickly began to work with Punjabi women and girls. She founded the orphanage and the Girls' Boarding School in Sialkot. In one reports it was written of her:

"She has during the year visited thirty villages, reading the Gospel to all classes, and faithfully and perseveringly teaching the Christians how to lead a Christian life; and she has done much to bring forward the heathen wives of Christians for baptism."

She continued her work in India for 45 years until 1900.

Ram Chand becomes Elisha Swift

Ram Chand was born in a Hindu home in 1824, one of five brothers. The oldest brother, Ram Bakhsh, joined the army and went to fight in Afghanistan. He died in Kabul.

Ram Chand was placed, together with two of his younger brothers, in the Presbyterian Mission orphanage in Ludhiana. There he became a follower of Jesus Christ and was given the name Elisha Swift.

In 1846 he left the orphanage and married a Christian girl from the orphanage called Salina Maria. He worked as an accountant in a government office before becoming head teacher in the mission school founded by Dr Charles Forman – and he opened a boys' school in Gujranwala with 100 students. His wife, Salina, became principal of a girls' school with 350 students. In 1856 he joined Andrew Gordon as a full-time evangelist. Wherever he went, he was always preaching the Gospel.

George Scott – evangelist

Elisha Swift's younger brother was given the name George Scott by the missionaries in the Christian orphanage. On 7th January 1859 they were the first two Indians to be ordained as pastors by the Presbyterian Church in Punjab.

George Scott was an orphan. In the Christian orphanage it was said that *"he was not inclined to study and sometimes behaved badly"* for which he was often punished. Lazy and undisciplined, he left the orphanage and almost died from hunger. It was a turning point in his life when one night, all alone in the jungle, he cried to God for mercy. God heard his prayer and restored him.

He went to work for a Muslim businessman who liked him – except that George Scott was a Christian and was always preaching to everyone he met. Nothing would silence him and so he lost his job. Then he met a British Army officer, Colonel Wheeler, who had received a lot of Bibles. George said: *"This is the Lord's work. I will take them to Kabul."*

Dost Mohammad Khan and his sons.
King of Afghanistan 1792–1863

On his way through Afghanistan, someone asked him: *"Who are you? What is your faith?"*

George confessed: *"I am a Christian. I am taking Bibles to Kabul. I know I am risking my life."*

On arriving in Kabul, King Dost Mohammad discovered what he was doing, and told him: *"Renounce your Christian faith and repeat the Muslim creed."* George refused. The king ordered him to discuss his faith with a learned mullah. George agreed. But the mullah (or *maulvi*) could not find any fault in his arguments. Finally, the king ordered that he should be taken to the border and returned to India.

The Sialkot Mission

Dr Andrew Gordon was joined in his work by George Scott and Elisha Swift. They formed a strong team with a passionate desire to evangelise the area around Sialkot. Dr Gordon's family escaped to Lahore, accompanied by George Scott, when the soldiers rebelled in Sialkot in June 1857. One month later they returned to Sialkot.

They found many houses destroyed or burned, and *"furniture, tents, clothing, books taken away or torn to pieces…"* However, their own mission houses were just as they had left them. Gordon was thankful for the protection of his *"All-wise Heavenly Father"*.

Andrew Gordon and his co-workers then began preparations to build a church – the first church building in Sialkot. It was a huge challenge to their faith as they had very little money.

They managed to purchase a plot of land costing 40 rupees ($20). With some help from the Government, the church opened on 14th August 1859. The total cost was 4,000 rupees *"all contributed in India".*

The first converts: Jauhari and Ram Bhajan

George Scott and Elisha Swift were both ordained as pastors in the Sialkot Mission of the Presbyterian Church in 1859. They were both active and zealous in evangelism, and before there was a church building, there were some converted Christians.

Jauhari was a very old man, a *Chuhra* (outcaste) who had spent his life in absolute poverty, doing the most simple servant tasks and subject to terrible treatment from the other caste Hindus.

> *"When one of the evangelists sat down in the hut of this poor old, grey-headed heathen, and told him the story of the Son of God, and that Jesus was the friend of the poor and willing to save just such sinners as he was, the old man received the Good News with great delight."*

At the same time an educated high-caste Hindu, **Ram Bhajan**, also received Christ as his Saviour. On 25th October 1857 the two men – the high-caste Hindu and the poor low-caste old man – stood up together, declared their faith in Christ and were baptised. Some of the missionaries were troubled, thinking that the conversion of a low-caste person might close the door for caste Hindus and Muslims. They need not have worried. Shortly after, a respected Muslim came to faith in Christ.

Andrew Gordon wrote of this great event: *"These were our first-fruits – an important and joyful event in our history – in the case of these first converts the power of the Gospel to bring down the proud and exalt the humble afforded us great encouragement."* In the following year 11 more people, both Hindus and Muslims, gave their lives to Jesus Christ.

Andrew Gordon and *Our India Mission*

Andrew Gordon opened an orphanage with three children. The Sialkot Mission School grew to 90 students, though many left when one of the Hindu students, Bal Krishan, became a Christian.

Dr Gordon had to return to America because of ill-health in 1885. What changes there had been since he first arrived in Sialkot! The young church that began with one Punjabi Christian, now 30 years later had a membership of 3,245. There were seven organised church congregations, and at least some Christians living in 200 villages.

Back in his home in America Andrew Gordon began to write the story of the Sialkot Mission. He died two years later on 13th August 1887. He closed his great book with these words:

"Judging from the number of converts, my last year in India was more fruitful by far than the first ten.

Having sown in tears, I have lived to see the plenteous harvest… what should hinder me now from reaping in joy, while yet able to do my humble share… May the word 'failure' never be written upon my latter days!

"Permit me now, dear reader, to ask you: are you doing your part – somewhere, somehow – in the great work?"

This is the book, written by Andrew Gordon in 1885, that tells the story of the first 30 years of the Sialkot Mission

The growth of the Sialkot Mission

In 1862 Rev. James Barr and his wife Mary arrived in Sialkot. She worked in the girls' orphanage, and in 1863 he moved to Gujranwala with George Scott to start boys' and girls' schools for non-Christians. The Christian Training Institute opened in 1881 and was intended for  Christians only, to prepare them for seminary studies. It was written that *"from this Institute thousands of boys have gone out to be ministers, teachers and leaders..."*

He was joined by Jiwan Mall, a Hindu who gave his life to Christ and was baptised. Jiwan studied and became pastor of the Presbyterian church in Gujranwala, and also head teacher in the Training Institute.

This is how James and Mary Barr travelled across India to Sialkot

Chapter 11

Spiritual Awakening Among the Meghs

The Meghs: "The great desire of our hearts"

About 30 miles east of Sialkot is a small town, Zafarwal. A few miles south of Zafarwal is a village called Jhandran. There lived 25 families of Meghs. A man called Mastan Singh came to the village and asked the villagers: *"Have you people ever found God?"*

"No, we have not found God," they replied. *"It is the very thing we are all looking for. This is the great desire of our hearts."*

Mastan Singh was an atheist. He did not believe in any God, and he could not help the villagers. However, a few months later a simple Christian evangelist called Jahawar Masih came to Jhandran. He met a crowd of villagers and began to read the Gospel of Mark to them.

When he had finished, he said: *"My brothers, you should repent and believe on the Son of God."* One replied: *"What wonderful words! This is the very thing we are all looking for."*

Who were the Meghs?

The Meghs are a caste in Hinduism. Many are still living in India. They are traditionally engaged in farming, cow-herding and weaving. They are known for beautiful embroidery and the textile industry.

They claim to have descended from "Rishi Megh", a saint who had the power to bring rain from the clouds through his prayer.

In 1860 there were about 600,000 Meghs in Punjab, many of them poor and illiterate.

Pipo, the first Megh Christian

George Scott came to Jhandran to teach the people. The first man to stand up and declare that he believed in Jesus was Pipo, a leader in his community. Eighty others followed his example.

Sadly, the new believers faced great opposition from both Hindus and Muslims in the village. They were threatened. They were not allowed to draw water from the wells belonging to Hindus and were not even allowed to share their carpets with Hindus. Many returned to their old faith, but Pipo remained faithful. He was beaten and thrown out of his village, but *"he had come to love Jesus with a love so strong that he could never turn back"*.

Pipo did not live for long. He fell ill in 1866. Knowing he was going to die, he called his family and his friends. *"We can meet again through Jesus Christ,"* he said, *"if you believe on Him."* His brother, Bhajna, accepted Christ as Saviour, as Pipo died and left the world to meet Jesus.

The conversion of Bhajna and Kanaya

George Scott, the evangelist, now took special care of Bhajna after Pipo's death. He visited him in his village – and then Bhajna walked 36 miles to visit Scott in Sialkot. *"I have come to visit you,"* he said, *"as you are, so am I, on Christ's side."* He faced great opposition from his community and from his family, but now Bhajna was determined to live for Christ.

Bhajna had a close friend called Kanaya. Kanaya was not well educated, having attended school for only 17 days, but he was quiet and determined also to become a Christian. *"With all my heart, Brother Bhajna,"* he said, *"I will go with you and be a Christian."*

They faced great opposition from their relatives and many friends. Their parents too refused to welcome them. They were beaten by mobs of angry Hindus, shouting: *"Beat them until they give up this religion."* To this they replied: *"If we were even to die for it, we will not leave Christ; and we desire that you also believe on Him; for if you do not, you cannot be saved."*

Bhajna was married, but his wife's family refused to allow her to join him unless he denied Christ and returned to his old religion. *"Only say 'I am not a Christian,' and take your wife and live happily among us!"* Bhajna could not accept this plea. *"I cannot deny the Lord Jesus Christ, who is Lord of heaven and of earth."* He moved to Sialkot to study theology and became a great preacher and evangelist. He married again – and happily his parents both received Christ and were baptised in 1876.

Bhajna (top left) and Kanaya (bottom right) with other evangelists

Kanaya and his estranged wife: Ramdei becomes Piyari

As the number of Christians increased, George Scott and the missionaries decided to purchase land close to Zafarwal and Jhandran. They called it Scottgarh. Kanaya and Bhajna built small houses and lived there together with seven Christian families, who became farmers on the land.

In 1867 Kanaya began a long struggle to try to persuade his wife, Ramdei, and their four children to join him. They refused, unless he agreed to renounce Christ and return to his old religion. Kanaya could not do that.

"It would be the same as to deny Christ," he said. *"We must take up our cross and follow Him. Kanaya can never turn back."* He decided to take the matter to the Deputy Commissioner's court. After many delays, the court ruled that Kanaya had won his case.

To Kanaya's great sadness, he then discovered that Ramdei and the four children had all been sent away to Kashmir. For several months Kanaya did not know where they were. He finally discovered that they were being kept safe by the Maharaja of Kashmir. *"Brethren,"* he said, *"I will go to Jammu, the capital of Kashmir, and present my petition to the King himself."*

Three times Kanaya travelled to Kashmir to plead for the release of his wife and family. He was determined and courageous, and ran many risks and dangers. Wherever he went, even among the Muslims of Kashmir, he continued to share his Christian faith boldly and to give away Gospels. Even before the King of Kashmir he shared the message of salvation without fear.

Finally, with help from the Government of India, Ramdei and the four children returned to Scottgarh. They were welcomed by Kanaya and all the excited Christians in the village. *"They have come!"* they cried. *"The children and Kanaya have come!"*

Ramdei became a Christian four years later and changed her name to Piyari (Beloved). They lived in Scottgarh, where Kanaya became a farmer and *Lambardar* (head man) of the village. Their seven children all became Christian evangelists and pastors' wives. Kanaya and Bhajna became elders in the first church in Scottgarh. Dr Andrew Gordon wrote: *"Scottgarh is now a small village, consisting of Christians only, some of the very happiest people I have met in all India."*

Kanaya loved to sing. His favourite song was Psalm 111: *"Praise the Lord. I will praise the Lord with my whole heart."* He died in Sargodha in 1911.

Chapter 12

Ditt and the Chuhra Revival

A Jat called Nattu

Not far from Zafarwal there lived a Hindu of the Jat caste, whose name was Nattu Lal. He heard the Gospel and put his faith in Christ. He was baptised in November 1872. Nattu was the son of the head man in his village. His family was wealthy, but Nattu wasted his money and proved himself to be a poor Christian witness. But one thing he did that was of great importance. He brought a poor *Chuhra* man called Ditt to faith in Jesus.

> **What was the Jat caste?**
>
> The Jats are mostly farmers living in Punjab. They were originally Hindus, though many converted to Islam or Sikhism. Many are wealthy land owners. Today there are many Muslim Jats living mostly in Baluchistan.

Ditt: the small man with a very big heart

Dr Gordon wrote in his book: *"In a village southwest of Mirali (near Zafarwal) there lived a man of the Chuhra tribe, by name Ditt, a dark little man, lame in one leg, quiet and modest, with sincerity in his face, at that time about thirty years of age."*

After telling him about Jesus, Nattu went with him to meet a missionary in Sialkot called Samuel Martin. Ditt immediately asked to be baptised. The missionary wanted him to stay and receive some teaching about his new faith, but Ditt did not want to stay. Samuel Martin baptised him and he immediately returned to his village, 30 miles away.

Back in his village Ditt began to tell his family and friends about Jesus. Some were angry. Some refused to listen. One person told him: *"You already have a broken leg; may your other also break!"*

Who were the *Chuhra*?

It is very sad that the word *"Chuhra"* has been used as an insult to describe Pakistan's Christians. No one likes to be called a *"Chuhra"*, as it is an unacceptable and insulting way of describing the followers of Christ as second-class citizens. Though many of Pakistan's Christians come from families that once belonged to the *"Chuhra"* caste in India's Hindu ancient caste system, many also come from Muslim or Sikh backgrounds and other Hindu castes.

Dr John O'Brian, a Catholic priest from Ireland, studied the origins of the *Chuhra* in Punjab. His book, **The Unconquered People**, traces the original inhabitants of Punjab to the Indus Valley Civilisation, which built Mohenjodaro and Harappa. When the Aryans invaded in about 1500 BC, they forced the people of Punjab to become their servants and slaves. They were the *Chandals* and became known as the *Chuhra* – and finally the lowest caste of the Hindu caste system.

The Aryans were victorious, and they treated the *Chuhra* badly – oppressing and forcing them to serve the new masters. O'Brian says: *"The fact that they survived the cruelest treatment ranks as one of the greatest triumphs of the human spirit... commemorated as a story of courage and not of shame."* The *Chuhra* were not a defeated people – they were proud of their origins as Punjab's original inhabitants. They enjoyed a rich culture of traditions, dances and music.

Many of the *Chuhra* became Christian and escaped from the cruel ways in which they were treated by the Aryans and other invaders of Punjab. Today's Pakistani Christians, if they come from a *Chuhra* family, should be proud of their inheritance. They are indeed the true owners and people of Punjab.

The courage of the little man of faith

While many of his family members mocked and criticised, Ditt continued to urge his friends and family to turn to Jesus. *"You may oppose me,"* he said, *"but your opposition will never induce me to deny Christ."*

Three months later, in August 1873, to his great joy, Ditt's wife and daughter and two of his near neighbours became Christians. Together they walked the 30 miles back to Sialkot where Mr Martin baptised them. They then all immediately returned to their village homes.

In February 1874, Ditt returned to Sialkot with four more men asking for baptism to become Christians. One of them, named Kaka, was the first male relative of Ditt to become a Christian. He became an active evangelist. He led two boys to Christ, followed by their fathers, who had up to then been strongly opposed to the Gospel. So these simple, desperately poor believers from the *Chuhra* caste became shining lights to their own community. Strong in faith, simple in testimony and determined in zeal – they formed the foundation of the Punjabi church of today.

From a social outcaste to a much loved teacher

In 1873, when Ditt was converted, he had never been to school and never learned to read or write. But his love for Christ and the example of his life were strong witness to the reality and truth of the Gospel message. Dr Gordon wrote this about him:

"When Ditt now visits his people, as he goes from place to place on his good work, their love to him and their joy at meeting him are as strong as once were their hatred and opposition."

Ditt used to say to those who had opposed him: *"Are you really the same people who used to be such enemies to me?"* And they replied: *"Whatever we did against you was ignorant and foolish. We did not know the excellence of the Christian religion."*

"When differences arise between Christian brethren, when advice is needed in regard to matters of religion, the Christians trustingly resort to Ditt as their wise and able counsellor."

Abdullāh,   Muhammad Alim,   Rahmat Masih,   Prem Masih,   Chaughattā.
John Clement,   Aziz-ul-Hakk,   Karm Dād,   Imām-ul-Din Shāhbaz,
Ditt.

**Ditt lying in front of other Christians and evangelists.
Note (*on the right*) Imam-ud Din Shahbaz from Zafarwal, who
wrote the Psalms in Punjabi that are still sung today.**

The spreading revival fire

Forty miles away, close to Gujranwala, in the same year as Ditt became
a Christian, another *Chuhra* accepted Christ and was baptised. His name
was Karim Bakhsh. In Gurdaspur (now in India), 45 miles away, two
other *Chuhra* were converted, Chaughatta and Prem Masih. God was
touching the hearts of the poor and drawing them to Himself in many
districts of Punjab.

After some opposition and open persecution, from 1873 many from the
poor among the *Chuhra* caste responded to the message of Christ. In a
quiet way, as these new converts shared the Gospel with friends and
family, the Holy Spirit began a work that would sweep thousands into the
Christian church.

Part 4

(Chapters 13 to 16)

From
Missionary Commitment (1850)
to
the Growing Church (1900)

Missionaries and Punjabi Christian believers

Chapter 13

1850–1900 : Churches and Missions

The Amazing growth of the church

After 1850 suddenly everything changed. We have seen what was happening in Sialkot with the Presbyterian Mission. In 1873 there were fewer than 200 Punjabis in Presbyterian churches. In 1900, 27 years later, there were more than 7,000. By 1930 there were 45,000 members of the United Presbyterian Church in Punjab. There was also a movement to Christ among the Khoja caste in Narowal.

There were new things happening all over Punjab and Sindh. The number of mission societies increased – the Roman Catholic missionaries, the Church Missionary Society, the Methodists and Church of Scotland, the Salvation Army, and many others. They opened schools, built churches and established hospitals.

The number of Punjabi Christians and church leaders increased. Many were active in evangelism, preaching, teaching and music. In this chapter we will look at just a few of those who made the greatest impact on the spread of the Christian community in the nineteenth century.

Churches built before 1900

The Church Missionary Society built and opened churches in Peshawar and Multan in 1853. This was how one person described the new church in Peshawar:

"On Thursday last were seen, for the first time in Peshawar, many leading chiefs reverently sitting behind the believers, and listening attentively to a Christian moulvi as he preached to them boldly and very plainly the Gospel of Christ. There was no opposition at all; the leading chief of the district was there...."

There were fewer Roman Catholic churches in Punjab and Sindh before 1900. **St Michael's Catholic Church** in Peshawar was consecrated in 1851. **St Anthony's Church**, Lahore, consecrated in 1899, is one of the oldest churches in the Roman Catholic Archdiocese of Lahore.

Well-known Pakistani churches

St Patrick's Cathedral, Karachi

The first church in Sindh, St Patrick's Church, was built in 1845 at a cost of 6,000 rupees. The city's Catholics then raised money for the construction of a new church. Ground breaking was done in 1878, and the

church was consecrated on 24th April 1881. The original small church was destroyed in a storm in 1885.

St Mary's Cathedral, Multan

The church was opened in 1848 to cater for the spiritual needs of British Army personnel posted at Multan. Sadly, it was neglected and fell into disrepair. It was closed for some time but restored by the Pakistan Army with the close collaboration of the citizens of Multan in 2016, at a cost of more than 5 million rupees.

Thomas Valpy French, the first Bishop of Lahore

Thomas French was born on 1st January 1825 in England. His father was a pastor who taught him to love the Bible and trust in Christ as his Saviour. After studying at university, he applied to the Church Missionary Society to serve overseas. He arrived in India in 1851.

He spent the next eight years in Agra near Delhi where he became fluent in Urdu, Punjabi and Persian. During the 1857 War of Independence, he refused to take refuge in Agra Fort, saying he would not leave his post *"unless all the Indian Christians are also given refuge in the fort"*. In this way the local Christians were also protected.

In 1861 he moved to Peshawar and in 1869 to Lahore. He loved to go into the bazaar to preach the Gospel. His second passion was teaching theology and training. In 1870 he founded the St John's Divinity School, Lahore, for the training of Indian Christian pastors.

St John's was opened in the former gardens of Ranjit Singh's father, Mahan Singh, purchased by Thomas French. It opened with four students, who soon increased to 11. French's vision of the college was clear:

"What we want for this school is that it should be a house of prayer – a home of prayerful, simple Bible students; a place where earnest intercession goes up night and day for the growth of Christ's Kingdom."

Students and staff at St John's Divinity School

In 1877 Thomas Valpy French was consecrated as the first Bishop of Lahore. One of his great achievements was the construction of the Cathedral Church of the Resurrection, which began in 1879 and was completed in 1887. The two towers were added in 1898, with two tall spires that were

removed after an earthquake in 1911 for safety reasons.

Bishop French finally left Lahore in 1887. He was always a restless evangelist, and continued to preach and distribute Bibles wherever he went in Arabia and Syria. He died on 14th May 1891 in Muscat, Oman, on the coast of Arabia. On his tomb are written the words: *"First Bishop of Lahore, and first Missionary to Muscat."*

Some of Pakistan's best-loved churches

Many churches were built across Punjab and Sindh after 1850. Most of the large churches were built to serve the British Army officers and soldiers, but increasing numbers of local Christians also attended. Most cities in Pakistan, from Peshawar to Karachi, now have several large church buildings. We can show only a few in this chapter.

All Saints Church, Peshawar

All Saints Church was opened in December 1883. It was described as a native Christian church built for the local people of Peshawar. The first pastor was the Rev. Imam Shah. Sadly, the church became famous in September 2013 when two suicide bombers carried out an attack outside the church at the

end of a Sunday service, killing 85 people and injuring 140.

St John's Church, Peshawar

St John's Church is the oldest church in that city, constructed between 1851 and 1860. It is now called the Cathedral Church of St John. It was built for the families of the soldiers stationed in the North-West Frontier. The photo was taken in 1878.

Holy Trinity Church, Karachi

Holy Trinity Church was built in 1855. It had a tower 150 feet tall. At the top of the tower lights were lit to help ships in the Karachi Harbour. In 1904 it was found that the foundation was weak and the top two stories of the tower were removed, reducing its height to 115 feet. The picture is how it looked in 1900.

Chapter 14

1850–1900 : Some Outstanding Missionaries, Pastors and Evangelists

I.D. Shahbaz and the Punjabi Psalms

Not far from the village where Nattu and Ditt lived, in Zafarwal, Sialkot District, a baby was born in 1844. Imam-ud-Deen Shahbaz was raised in a Muslim family, but from the age of ten was attracted to the Christian message. He accepted Jesus Christ and was baptised by Robert Clark in 1876. He was also a gifted teacher, serving at CMS schools in Amritsar and being engaged in evangelistic activities from 1876 to 1880.

In 1880 the Presbyterian Church announced a poetry competition in their magazine, *Noor Afshan*. Many scholars and writers wrote poems, but I.D.

Shahbaz was declared the winner. He was invited by the Church to begin translating the Psalms into the Punjabi language. For I.D. Shahbaz this became his lifelong passion and a source of untold blessing to millions of Punjabi speaking Christians.

He was first asked to translate the Psalms into Urdu for singing in church. Only when that work was completed, and the Urdu Psalter turned out not to be very popular with the Punjabi village congregations, was he asked to translate them into Punjabi poetry. He then set the Punjabi Psalms to popular folk tunes with the help of some Indian musicians and missionaries. One of his helpers, Henrietta Cowden, wrote down how they worked together:

"An Indian, Radha Kishan, a professional Hindu singer, was found who agreed to give time... He went to Dr Shahbaz, who had already prepared some of the poems. The two would read the poem together until the singer caught the rhythm, then he would fit a tune to that rhythm and metre, and come back to Dr Shahbaz and sing it to him.

I then wrote it and sang it to him. If he approved, it was ready to go to the printers. If not satisfactory, then it had to be corrected."

He moved to Gurdaspur, where he worked with Andrew Gordon, as well as taking part in evangelistic activities. He was ordained as a pastor by the United Presbyterian Church in Sialkot.

In later years he gradually became blind, but his work continued. He was helped by another Punjabi pastor. *"Often he would lie in his bed with his head completely covered while Babu Sadiq read to him."* A missionary, Anna Milligan, wrote about him: *"Padri I. D. Shahbaz, the poet, grown old and blind, put the Psalms into Punjabi verse and thus made them the most popular songs of the whole Church of Christ in the Punjab."*

Today the *Zabur* (Psalms) are sung everywhere where Urdu or Punjabi Christians congregate to worship.

The Rev. Mawlawi Dr Imad ud-Din Lahiz

Imad ud-Din Lahiz was born in 1830 in Panipat, India. His father, grandfather and great-grandfather had all been *maulvis* and Islamic scholars. They were all zealous for the Muslim faith.

Imad ud-Din had also written many books about the history, faith and practices of Islam and had also translated the Qur'an into Urdu. In 1854 he attended a large meeting in Agra, in which a well-known Islamic scholar, Rahmatullah Kairanawi, debated the Muslim and Christian faiths with the German Christian, Karl Gottlieb Pfander. Dr Imad ud-Din was there to support the Muslim faith.

He later wrote: *"I was filled with zeal for the cause of Islam. I began to recite the Qur'an throughout the night. I considered Christianity to be worthless..."* But he was troubled by the strong reasons given by Dr Pfander for the truth of the Christian faith. From Agra he travelled to Lahore where he met several Christians, Rev. Guru Das, Robert Clark and Dr Charles Forman. He began to read the Gospel of Matthew.

He had a growing fear of death and no peace in his heart or mind. He even thought about killing himself, but as he read he came to know that the Lord Jesus Christ was the Truth who alone could give him peace and salvation.

> *"Ever since I have entered into the grace of the Lord Jesus Christ, I have had much spiritual satisfaction... No longer do I experience great anxiety of heart. Through the reading of God's Word I have found great pleasure in life and I am wonderfully happy in the Lord.*
> *The Lord gives peace of heart."*

Dr Imad ud-Din converted to Christianity and was baptised at Amritsar on 29th April 1866 together with his aged father, his brother, his wife, five sons and four daughters. He faced much criticism and opposition from his former friends. He joined the Church Missionary Society and became a powerful preacher of the Gospel. He wrote ten books, including his own story. Through his testimony he brought many people to faith in Christ.

Karl Gottlieb Pfander

(1803–1865)

Dr Pfander was a German missionary in Central Asia. He studied Islam and learned many central Asian languages, including Arabic and Persian.

He arrived in India in 1838 and lived in Agra. He moved to Peshawar in 1855, continuing to preach until 1857 when he left India and moved to Istanbul.

He is well known for entering into great debates with Muslim scholars. He translated several books on Islam and Christianity into Urdu. He then wrote a book that was translated into many languages, **Mizan-ul Haq**, that compares the teachings of Christianity and Islam.

Missionaries, pastors and evangelists

As the number of missionaries increased, so did the number of local converts, many of whom became the best evangelists and finest pastors of growing churches across Punjab, Sindh and the North-West Frontier. Here is a brief insight into the lives of a few:

Missionaries from the Church of Scotland, together with several national pastors and evangelists. The photo is from about 1890.

Muhammad Ismail and his wife, Sally

Muhammad Ismail met Thomas Hunter in Bombay and began to teach him Urdu. His life was changed when he received Christ as his Saviour. *"Under the power of the Word of God, he became a man of wise zeal, self-sacrifice and devoted piety."* He joined Hunter and moved to Sialkot in 1856. He was ordained and became pastor of the Hunter Memorial Church. He sadly died in 1873.

Muhammad's wife Sally became active in work with the women, which continued after her husband's death. She took meetings with the Muslim women every Sunday. It was reported that *"they have begun to take interest in hearing the Scriptures"*. Sally was a true and zealous evangelist among the women in Sialkot.

Rev. John F. W. Youngson and his co-workers

Rev. John Youngson came from a village of fishermen in Scotland. He married Helen in 1875 and they became missionaries with the Church of Scotland.

They arrived in Punjab two years later. He served faithfully in Gujrat and Daska, visited 100 villages in which he was assisted by one of his converts, Didar Singh. Youngsonabad is named in honour of John Youngson.

Didar Singh (photo *right* with his family) from Gujrat, a former Sikh, was baptised by Rev. Youngson in 1878. He married a Christian girl, Isabella, and worked alongside John Youngson as an evangelist.

Hakim Singh (left *above*), standing with Rev. Youngson) was a Sikh convert to Christianity who became the pastor of a small community of Christians in Wazirabad.

Archdeacon Ihsan Ullah (1858–1929)

Ihsan Ali was one of three brothers in a high-class Shia family of the Khoja caste in Narowal. He decided to follow Christ and was baptised in 1878, at which time he changed his name to Ihsan Ullah. He was also influenced by the Salvation Army, which sent him to England for training in 1883. He was ordained as a priest by the Bishop of Lahore in 1895.

Rev. Ihsan Ullah became the Church Missionary Society pastor at Narowal in 1891 until 1909. He took part in the crowning of King George V as King-Emperor in the Delhi Darbar of 1911.

He was a gifted evangelist and pastor. He first visited England together with William Booth of the Salvation Army in 1883, and in 1898 he spoke at the CMS Centenary meeting in London and at the Royal Albert Hall. In America he met the great evangelist D.L. Moody. God used him powerfully in the revival of 1896. Together with the missionary, John Hyde, he was one of the founders of the Sialkot Convention in 1904.

In 1911 Bishop Lefroy made him Archdeacon of Delhi, responsible for the spiritual life of all the Indian churches in the diocese. He was the first Indian to attain such a high position. He retired from ministry in 1923, and died in Multan in 1929, aged 72.

The Delhi Durbar of 1911, at which King George V was acknowledged as King-Emperor of India. Archdeacon Ihsan Ullah took part in the ceremony.

Missionaries and pastors together

This photo of the clergy of the Anglican Diocese of Lahore was taken at the Consecration of Bishop Lefroy on All Saints Day, 1899

(The photo is from the blogspot of Jol Martyn Clark)

Robert Clark concluded his memoir with these words:

"We who are missionaries in India have need of humiliation and confession. Missionaries are in no ways perfect. We are only sinful men and women, acting according to the grace which we have received... The time may be very near when this people in the Punjab and Sindh will offer themselves willingly for this work...

And then will the song of praise burst forth again from His obedient people: 'Thine, O Lord, is the greatness, and the power, and the glory, and the victory, and the majesty: for all that is in the heaven and in the earth is Thine...'

Yes, then will come the rejoicing and the blessing. The Lord will Himself enter into His temple, which His servants have built for Him. The people will then be His people, and God Himself shall be their God. May God hasten it in His own time."

Chapter 15

1850–1900 : Christian Schools and Hospitals

The schools and Christian education

Before the mass movement of *Chuhras* to Christianity, most missionaries were not working much among the poor. Many missions opened schools for upper-class students, high-caste Hindus, Sikhs and Muslims. They believed schools would be able to teach the Christian faith, with Bible teaching an essential part of the curriculum. This policy changed after the mass conversion. Missionaries felt the need to educate their converts to improve their lives as Christians.

Karachi Grammar School was opened by the First Chaplain of Karachi, Henry Brereton, in 1847. The school began in his own home, and the first classes were held in his kitchen. It then moved to the Methodist church while the initial building was being constructed. It moved into its own buildings in 1875 and changed its name to the Karachi Grammar School four years later. It is still one of Karachi's finest schools.

St Patrick's High School in Karachi opened in 1861. It began with just three students, and officially registered as a high school in 1867. Its founder was Reverend Joseph Willy of the Society of Jesus.

For the last 150 years, the school has produced well-known leaders and public

The old School Building, 1891–1918.

figures, including two presidents and two prime ministers of Pakistan, two chief ministers of Sindh, one deputy prime minister and two cardinals of the Catholic Church.

The Christian Training Institute, Sialkot

The Girls' Boarding School at Hajipur, Sialkot, started as an orphanage in 1857. In 1879 it became a small day-school for Hindu girls, and then a boarding school for Christian girls. It was run very simply in keeping with the village background of the students. They studied on mats on the floor and took turns to cook their usual diet of dal and roti. The CTI High School, Barah Pather, Sialkot, founded in 1881, still serves young people from all communities. It has produced doctors, engineers, judges and army men.

By 1880 11 Christian high schools had been opened across Punjab and Sindh. Middle and primary schools were also opened in many cities. In total by 1880, there were 120 Christian schools in Punjab, with about 9,000 students.

Mission hospitals – healing the sick

Dr Theodore Pennell of Bannu

Dr Pennell was born in England in 1867. He qualified as a doctor in 1890 and immediately applied to the Church Missionary Society. He sailed with his mother to Karachi, arriving in 1892. They travelled on to Dera Ismail Khan, where Pennell began medical work. He often travelled round the villages wearing Pathan dress and living with the people. He made his first visit to Tank in 1893. He was fluent in Urdu and Pushtu and began to preach to the local tribal people. He faced immediate opposition from the mullahs, but he continued to preach.

The CMS mission school in Bannu opened in 1865. Thirty years later Dr Pennell and his mother revitalised it. They took a keen interest in the school and it became a high school in 1898. A hostel was built for boys from tribal territory to attend.

He also built a small hospital at Bannu with his mother's money, starting with a few patients. By 1896 there were 28 beds. This medical ministry broke down many barriers and promoted the sharing of the Gospel.

In 1908 he married a Christian doctor, Dr Alice Sorabji, whose father had converted to Christianity. The husband and wife team worked together in the hospital. Dr Pennell sadly died in 1912, but Dr Alice remained in charge of the hospital at Bannu until her retirement in 1925. She lived until 1951 and was awarded the *Kaiser-e-Hind* medal for Public Service.

The Bannu Mission Record Book gives brief profiles of those who professed faith in Christ. Between 1876 and 1897 21 converts are noted. They faced much opposition from the local community. The Pennell Memorial Christian Hospital is still open in Bannu.

Christian hospitals throughout Punjab

In the following few years hospitals and clinics opened in many parts of Punjab, the North-West Frontier and Baluchistan. In 1899 the Church Missionary Society opened a special hospital for women in Multan. In the next 15 years, the CMS Mission recorded that *"Medical Missions formed a large part of their work. Christian hospitals were opened in Amritsar, Multan, Srinagar, Islamabad, Peshawar, Bannu, Dera Ismail Khan and Quetta. They had a total of 750 beds and 10,700 in-patients, in addition to many thousands of out-patients."*

Robert and Elizabeth Clark

The name of Robert Clark is well known, as he founded the village of Clarkabad in 1900. What is not so well known is his life as a missionary in Punjab, Afghanistan and Kashmir – and the courage of his wife Elizabeth.

Robert Clark was born, raised and educated in England. He arrived in Punjab in 1851 as a missionary with the Church Missionary Society. Together with several Punjabi evangelists and co-workers, he started preaching in the bazaar in Amritsar (now in India). He baptised 23 people who wanted to become Christian. He also opened a girls' school and a college in 1854.

"Our missionary policy should always be that we (the Europeans) must decrease, they (the Indians) must increase."

He then moved to Peshawar and Afghanistan for the next ten years. In 1858 he married Elizabeth from Scotland, the daughter of a missionary doctor. She spoke five languages including Urdu.

Robert Clark was convinced that medical ministry, the opening of hospitals and clinics, was the best way to serve the people and share the Gospel of Christ. *"Medical Missions are among the most important means of evangelising India,"* he wrote.

The Maharajah of Kashmir did not welcome the missionaries, and they faced constant opposition. He gave instructions to the police to keep away when their house was besieged by a howling mob of men and boys who threw stones and attacked their compound.

However, Mrs Elizabeth Clark was not discouraged. She was not a highly qualified doctor, but she knew more than the native *hakims* (local quacks). Hundreds of women, who would have died of simple illness, came to consult her. She opened the first clinic – and then a hospital – in Srinagar, the capital of Kashmir, and became the doctor of the city. Crowds came to consult her, 100 patients every day. Mr Clark was welcomed as a teacher.

Elizabeth Clark was joined later by other doctors and medical personnel. It has been said that the ministry of medical aid to the sick through the church in Punjab is the result of the efforts of Robert and Mrs Clark.

After Mrs Clark started basic health facilities in Srinagar, the people sometimes brought the sick to the hospital in houseboats on the Jhelum River that runs through Srinagar. This photograph is from 1872.

Robert Clark decided against retiring. *"I am not fit for much now, certainly not for travelling. I should only get ill, and be a burden, whilst doing no good and getting none myself. My heart clings to Mission work and to the workers."*

He died on 16th May 1900 in Kasauli near Simla. His last words were: *"I am very tired; let me sleep, for Jesus Christ's sake. We must, with much tribulation, enter into life."*

Chapter 16

Christian Communities and the Canal Colonies

Where should all these Christians live?

The number of Christian families was increasing rapidly, both through the missionaries and the effectiveness of their Punjabi evangelists. Unfortunately, many new Christians were not made welcome by their old, mainly Hindu, communities. Where should they live, so that they could continue to develop and be free to worship as Christians? One of the first to solve this problem was Robert Clark (see the last chapter).

Robert Clark of Clarkabad

In 1868 Robert Clark went to the Government of Punjab and asked if he could buy some land. The Government was willing to co-operate, and offered more than 2,000 acres about 30 miles south of Lahore, close to the Bari Doab Canal.

They agreed to rent the land in the name of four Punjabi Christians on certain conditions. The main condition was that within ten years the land would be cultivated and able to produce a good harvest. Robert Clark agreed and several families came to occupy the land – sadly none of them was a Christian and none of them was a farmer. After ten years they had not been successful or made any money from their rented land.

Another missionary, Roland Bateman, agreed to guarantee change in the village within the next five years. The first baptism in Clarkabad took place in November 1876. The next baptism was about a year later, and in the next 11 years, nearly 300 people were baptised. Work on the new church was completed in 1881 together with a mission house and boys' school – then a girls' school. Houses were built and rented for 1 rupee a month. Roads were built, 2,000 trees planted and a clinic was run by a Christian doctor, Abdul Rahim Khan. Within a few years the village was completely Christian.

In gratitude it was agreed to name the village Clarkabad in honour of its founder, Robert Clark.

Roland Bateman and Montgomerywala

As the number of Christians increased, the work began to care for them, build churches and give teaching to the new believers. Roland Bateman gave his life to this task. In 1899 he wrote: *"There had been great development in the irrigation from the Chenab Canal. A number of new villages had been settled by immigrants from the east, and a Christian village had been started at Montgomerywala in the middle of the Jhang Bar."* This was the beginning of the famous Chak 424, named after Sir Robert Montgomery, the Lieutenant Governor of the Punjab.

The Canal Colonies

Punjab is a large area with huge resources, largely because of the five rivers that flow from the mountains in the north: the Sutlej, Beas, Ravi, Chenab and Jhelum Rivers. There is plenty of water, which is essential for growing rice and wheat. And yet much of the land in western Punjab was dry and barren and not good for agriculture.

In about 1880 the Punjab Government began work on creating a network of canals to bring water to the huge areas of barren land. There were two reasons for the amazing plan:

1. To create living space and farm work on the land for new communities.
2. To create new villages to bring prosperity to the people and wealth to the Government.

Many new canals were dug between the major rivers. Each canal developed into a colony with new villages. Between the years 1885 and 1940, nine canal colonies were developed in the western Punjab between Gujranwala and Multan. The new canals increased and brought water to many parts of western Punjab.

The Government then offered land to thousands of people to build communities and start small self-supporting farms. Large areas of Punjab were made available to hard-working people to form new villages and bring greater prosperity. People who were given land in the colonies had to construct wells to mature the winter crops, and for this they had to have a certain amount of money to invest. To attract such people the minimum size of grants was fixed at 50 acres.

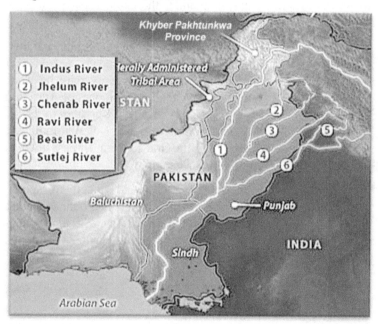

Dr Samuel Martin of Martinpur

Dr Samuel Martin was the missionary who baptised Ditt in 1873 (see Chapter 12). He and his wife Lydia arrived in Sialkot in 1867. Lydia Martin raised five daughters and two sons, and yet was fully active in ministry and evangelism. She died in 1886 in Zafarwal. *"No one was more capable, more devoted."*

Samuel Martin continued his work. In 1898, when the Chenab Canal was opened, he applied for land to form a village for Christians. It began with 72 families willing to build a house and start farming. It was named Martinpur in honour of its founder.

Rev. John Youngson of Youngsonabad

Less than two miles from Martinpur and in the same year 1898, Rev. John Youngson (see Chapter 14) founded the village of Youngsonabad.

Bakht Singh was born to Hindu parents in Punjab, and he was raised as a Sikh. After graduating from Punjab University he went to England and Canada as a student of Agricultural Engineering. He became a Christian in 1929 and four years later returned to Colonial India with a clear call from God to be a witness for Christ among his own people.

In June 1937 he was invited to speak at Youngsonabad. Though both Youngsonabad and Martinpur were known as Christian villages, there was much immorality, church in-fighting, jealousy and hatred everywhere. Bakht Singh agreed to come.

For four days he preached in Youngsonabad, but nothing happened until the final night. Then revival came. People began to cry out to God: *"Oh, Lord, have mercy on me: I am a sinner."* This continued for four hours. The people wept and wept till 3 am, repenting of their sins. The work of God continued for a whole week. So the blessing of God came to Youngsonabad and to Martinpur.

In 1937 he spoke at the Sialkot Convention from Luke 24:5 – *"Why seek ye the living among the dead?"* His preaching electrified the congregation and many were touched by the power of God.

Maryamabad and Khushpur

In January 1893 a Catholic Capuchin friar set out with a group of desperately poor Punjabi Christians to establish Maryamabad on a 126-acre plot given by the Government on the Chenab Canal.

When they arrived they constructed huts from tree branches and mud on the bare land that had never been cultivated. Many became ill from dysentery and malaria. Despite their hardship the Christians, led by two priests named Father Jacob and Father Felix, did not give up.

Father Felix from Belgium (centre)

They stayed and they built, and by 1900 the colony had prospered. It had real homes, a church and Mission Centre, and they had purchased 500 acres more land. Many Christian arrived and a new colony had to be established, which became known as Khushpur in honour of Father Felix (Felix is a Latin word, which means Happy or *Khushi* in Urdu).

Khushpur is the birthplace and last resting place of two great Pakistani martyrs, Bishop John Joseph (died in 1998) and Shahbaz Bhatti (murdered in 2011 – see Chapter 28).

Part 5

(Chapters 17 to 20)

From
Growing Church (1900)
to
Established Church (1947)

Changing times – the motor car overtakes the tonga

Chapter 17

Spiritual Revival in Punjab

The Revival of 1896

William Booth began his evangelical ministry in the poorest areas of London in 1865. He established mission stations to feed and house the poor. In 1878 he changed the name of his organisation to the Salvation Army. Five years later the Salvation Army came to Punjab.

In February 1896, General William Booth visited India and held meetings for spiritual renewal in Amritsar. His interpreter was a pastor from Narowal, Ihsan Ullah (see Chapter 14). On Saturday evening, as General Booth spoke against sin, Ihsan Ullah felt so convicted of pride in his own ministry that he began to weep. He rededicated his life to the Lord that night after the meeting, and pledged himself to fully obey the Holy Spirit.

On Sunday morning Ihsan Ullah publicly shared his experience with his church in Narowal. In response, many confessed their faults and asked forgiveness of one another. They left the service filled with a new power and joy. Revival spread from there.

The Salvation Army in Lahore

The Salvation Army began its work in Lahore in 1883. Commissioner Fredrick Booth-Tucker asked Captain Victoria Roberts to pioneer a work in Lahore. Roberts agreed, taking three assisting officers with her. They began in a small facility at Delhi Darwaza, a gate of the walled city. As everywhere, the Salvation Army focused on evangelism and aid to the poor.

A new Pentecost

A few days later Ihsan Ullah met two seminary students, Mallu Chand and Labhu Mall. He had known them since they were children. With great concern, he asked them, *"Brothers, are you saved?"* They were angry. *"Yes,"* they said – but then they suddenly felt convicted of sin and broke down in tears. They returned to the seminary changed men, and shared their experience with the other ten students, who spent that night getting right with God. Their wives were very surprised to hear the sound of weeping and wondered what was going on, but the next day, they also experienced a time of humble confession and renewal.

On 24th March 1896, the staff of the Sialkot churches met in Pasrur to study the first two chapters of Acts. At the end, the speaker urged them to accept the gift of the Holy Spirit. Immediately some of them fell to the ground and began to weep. They spent several hours in earnest prayer and confession of sin and afterwards they felt a deep joy and spirit of praise.

Prayer for the Holy Spirit to bring revival

Ihsan Ullah, together with many of the missionaries, were praying for a new work of the Holy Spirit among the growing numbers of Christians in the Sialkot area. Dr James Barr (see Chapter 10) began to preach on the importance of prayer to bring revival. Kanaya and his family were there and were stirred to pray.

Renewal in the Girls' Boarding School in Sialkot

One evening some of the girls met together to pray. Maryam, the youngest daughter of Kanaya, said: *"Sisters, let us sing Psalm 51, prayerfully, every head bowed."*

> *"Wash me wholly from my sins,*
> *Cleanse me from my guilty stains."*

Maryam continued to lead: *"Let us ask God's Holy Spirit to show us clearly where we have failed to overcome sin today."* Several girls began to weep and confess sins. Two girls confessed that they had stolen something from the store room.

Some of the older girls also began to confess their failures and to pray for forgiveness. Martha in Class 8, Isri and Hannah confessed their anger, bad temper and selfishness. *"If anyone is in Christ, he is a new creature,"* Maryan quoted from the Bible. *"My dear sisters, let us pray until God pours out His Holy Spirit on us."* One girl, Nasiban, had never given her life to Christ, but on that night at midnight she broke down. *"Sisters, rejoice with me,"* she said. *"Your prayers are answered. I have given my heart to Jesus."*

The Girls' Boarding School was established in 1892 by the Presbyterian Women's Association for Foreign Missions. The aim of the Association was to extend access for women to education and health care.

Mallu Chand and Labhu Mall

One evening Mallu Chand and Labhu Mall, two seminary students whose lives were changed through the Rev. Ihsan Ullah, wanted to hold a meeting in the boys' boarding hostel at the Christian Training Institute in Sialkot. The director of the hostel refused them permission, as he was afraid of what might happen when the Holy Spirit touched their young lives with new zeal.

Labhu Mall
(*right* with another pastor)

That night Labhu Mall said a special prayer: *"O Lord, please grant that this place, where we were forbidden to speak tonight, may become the centre from which great blessings shall flow to all parts of India."* His prayer was wonderfully answered because later the famous Sialkot Convention would take place in the same compound at the Training Institute.

The Sialkot Convention

In the years between 1896 and 1904 a few missionaries, local pastors and Indian seminary students were longing for the church to be revived with the fullness of the Holy Spirit. This led to the birth of the Punjab Prayer Union, and plans for a convention to be held in Sialkot in 1904.

Three missionaries, R. M'Cheyne Paterson, John Hyde and George Turner, prayed for 30 days before the convention started. They were joined by Pastor Ihsan Ullah and many others, including the 80-year-old Kanaya Lal. They prayed night and day for a mighty outpouring of the power of God. John Hyde committed himself to many hours of prayer, not only during but also after the convention. He became known as Praying Hyde because of the many hours he gave himself to prayer.

The 1904 Sialkot Convention was a revival meeting and many churches were touched by the blessing that followed. Three hundred missionaries and Indian pastors took part in the convention. Many lives were transformed.

The Sialkot Convention 1904

John Hyde – Praying Hyde

In 1892 a young Bible school graduate, John Hyde, left his home in America to travel to India. He had already begun to study Urdu. And yet, when he was told that he needed most of all to be filled with the Holy Spirit, he proudly reacted in anger.

After a few days of struggle, John had to admit that this friend was right and he surrendered to God, saying:

"I asked the Lord to fill me with the Holy Spirit, and the moment I did this, the whole atmosphere seemed to clear up… I was determined that, whatever would be the cost, I would be really filled with the Spirit."

Hyde began leading his fellow missionaries to pray for India. So deep was his call to prayer that by 1899 he began spending entire nights face down before God in prayer. In a letter to his college he wrote:

"I have felt led to pray for others this winter as never before. I never before knew what it was to work all day and then pray all night before God for another. In college or at home, I used to keep such hours for myself, or pleasure, and can I not do as much for God and souls?"

Together with others, John Hyde founded the Sialkot Convention. Hyde spent most of his time in the prayer room. His prayer life was closely linked to his passion for evangelism. It was a time of great spiritual harvest. *"Give me souls, oh God, or I die!"*

He returned to America in 1911, and a malignant tumour was discovered in his brain. He died there after an operation, in February 1912, aged 46. His final words were: *"Shout the victory of Jesus Christ!"*

Chapter 18

1900–1947 : Growing Churches Everywhere

The Revival that touched thousands

The Sialkot Convention of 1904 was the first such meeting. It was the beginning of a movement that continues until today. Conventions are now an important tradition for many churches all across Pakistan.

At the second Sialkot Convention, which took place for ten days in August 1905, 300 Punjabi believers were present, and a few missionaries. The prayer rooms were full throughout the meetings. Some people spent whole nights there, praying for God's blessing.

At the 1908 Sialkot Convention, 2,000 people attended. God put a special burden on John Hyde's heart: *"I have other sheep…"* He started to pray that he would bring one person to faith in Christ every day. At the 1909 Convention he prayed to lead two people to Christ every day – and at the 1910 Convention he began to lead four people to faith every day.

The Prayer Room in Hunter Memorial Church, Sialkot

"For a long time, one after another rose to his feet to pray. There was such confession of sin as most of us had never heard before and such crying out to God for mercy and help. It was very late that night when the gathering broke up."

"There was freedom during those ten days that I never imagined existed on earth. Surely it was for freedom such as this that Christ has set us free. Some went to bed early, some prayed all night long."

Growth of the Presbyterian churches

By 1910 there were 80 missionaries and other foreigners of the United Presbyterian Church in Sialkot, Gujranwala, Rawalpindi and Lyallpur (now Faisalabad), Jhelum and Sargodha. The number of Punjabi workers had grown to 662, including 34 ordained pastors, Bible women, teachers and theological students. In that one year 2,986 adults were baptised, most of them in Lyallpur and Sargodha. The church was growing fast!

There were two great institutions in the work of the Presbyterian Church: The Christian Training Institute (CTI) was opened in 1881, and prepared students for the Theological Seminary, which opened with 20 students in 1877. Both were in Sialkot.

Ministry in a motor car

This photo shows two Presbyterian missionaries, Dr David Gordon, Dr McCounelee and a local pastor, Rev. Mallu Chand (see Chapter 17), setting out for evangelism in their car in about 1910.

The Roman Catholic missions

Roman Catholic missionaries arrived at the court of Emperor Akbar in Agra in 1580 (see Chapter 5). For the next 50 years they preached, some people were converted and a few churches were established. Then it all closed own under Emperor Shah Jahan.

Roman Catholic mission work began again in Sindh in 1844 when priests came as chaplains to the British Army. St Patrick's Church was built in 1845 as a Carmelite mission. It cost 6,000 rupees and was led by Karachi's first Carmelite priest, Father Casaboch. Father Joseph A. Willy of the Society of Jesus opened St Patrick's School in 1861.

Karachi was an important centre for the Roman Catholic Church, with a large community of Catholics who had moved from the former Portuguese colony of Goa, south of Bombay. Outreach work in Kotri and Shikarpur was carried out and priests were stationed in Kotri from 1864. From 1882 priests were stationed in Sukkur for outreach in Shikarpur and

Larkana. The first priest arrived in Lahore in 1846. They opened orphanages in Lahore and Sialkot. The Sisters of Jesus and Mary came to Sialkot in 1855 to set up a convent and girls' school.

The Lahore Diocese was established in 1886 and the Cathedral of the Sacred Heart was built in 1907. The Jesus and Mary Sisters from France established the school and Convent of Jesus and Mary in both Murree (see the photo) and Lahore in 1876. St Anthony's School was opened in 1892

by the Capuchin friars from Belgium.

Growth in the community

Six Roman Catholic priests were working in Sialkot when the mass movement began among the *Chuhras* (see Chapter 12). By 1900, when thousands had been baptised in Presbyterian churches, there were only 1,500 Catholic Christians in the whole of Punjab.

Then things began to change. The Roman Catholic community grew to 8,000 in the next ten years. By 1931 there were more than 45,000 and by the time of Pakistan's Independence (1947) more than 120,000. The Catholics laid more stress on educational, medical and social work. They set up schools and clinics to raise the Christians out of their poverty and illiteracy.

The Roman Catholic Bible

Bishop Anastasius Hartmann from Switzerland arrived in India in 1843. His translation of the New Testament into Urdu was used by Catholics in India and Pakistan until 1959.

The Comity Agreement to co-operate

When the Government of India finally agreed to welcome missionaries, many churches and mission societies arrived and began to evangelise. They built churches and opened hospitals and schools. The first to arrive were the American Presbyterians (1834). Then came the Roman Catholics (1844) and the Church Missionary Society (1851), the Church of Scotland (1855), the Methodists (1880) – and many others.

To avoid the problems of competition, in December 1862 the leaders of several Protestant missions met in Lahore to discuss how they could co-operate better. It was called the Punjab Missionary Conference, a significant meeting of major mission societies to agree the way forward together, to co-operate and to support, and not to hinder or compete for converts or church members.

It was called a "Comity Agreement" – or an agreement to work together in harmony. The 398-page book of papers resulted in *"the adoption of some particular measures, by which it is hoped that the way may be opened for enabling the Christian public to cooperate more effectively than heretofore, in the work of missions, whereby the hands of the missionary brethren may be greatly strengthened, their labours lightened, and their minds relieved"*.

By 1900 more mission societies had arrived: the Salvation Army (1883), the Brethren (1897), the Lutherans (1903) the Associate Reformed Presbyterians (1906) and the Seventh-day Adventists (1913) and more. The Roman Catholics and most of the new missions did not observe the "Comity Agreement".

The Church Missionary Society

Rev. Walter P. Hares was a missionary with the Church Missionary Society. He arrived in Gojra in 1916 and started working to develop the Christian community. He lived very simply, had no car or other vehicle, and never lost his love for ordinary poor people.

Rev. Hares constructed the church in Batemanabad. He himself brought the bricks and worked as a labourer in church construction. It was built in 52 days in 1928.

When Walter Hares arrived to take charge of the district in December 1916, he found three large congregations in Gojra, Batemanabad (Issa Nagri) and Montgomerywala. By 1933, there were 250 Christian congregations connected to the Church Missionary Society (Anglican) church in the districts of Jhang and Toba Tek Singh, all of them formed from converts of low-caste origin. Rev. Hares made plans for 12 primary schools in the villages, a large hostel and school for boys in Gojra and a boarding school for girls.

> **Rev. Walter P. Hares**
>
> Rev. Hares wrote a book called *Joy in the Wilderness.*
>
> *"Once I was on a survey of a school in Gojra. Two children were sitting outside the class in an extremely hot summer afternoon. I asked them: 'Why are you sitting outside?' They replied: 'We are Christian and other children are Hindu and Muslim, so the teacher has separated us from them.' I called the teacher and told him that all humans are equal and such kind of behaviour is shameful."*

The Methodist Mission:
Dr and Mrs Clyde Stuntz

Dr and Mrs Clyde Stuntz arrived in Lahore in 1915. They were sent to serve as Methodist missionaries and they began their work in Raiwind. Some Christian villagers in central Punjab

invited Dr and Mrs Stuntz to their village. They worked hard to improve the lives of the Christian community. In gratitude they named their village Stuntzabad. About 20,000 people now live in Stuntzabad, mostly Christian farm labourers.

The Methodist missionary Dr John Butcher proposed starting a girls' school in Lahore. It was opened in 1912 by Miss Lily Greene in a two-room building with only 25 girls, and named the Lucie Harrison Girls' School. By 1920 the numbers had increased to 106, as parents took an increasing interest in the education of their girls. Dr Butcher also designed the first church building of the Central Church on Waris Road in Lahore.

The Zenana Bible and Medical Mission

The Zenana Bible and Medical Mission was born in 1880 out of the Indian Female Normal School and Instruction Society, founded in 1852 in England. It opened the door for single lady missionaries to work in Asia and became closely linked to the Church Missionary Society. Elizabeth Bielby was one of their first missionaries in Punjab. After founding a hospital in central India, she then directed the hospital in Lahore, known from 1887 as the Lady Aitchison Hospital for Women. She worked at the hospital for 15 years.

Among the supporters of the Zenana Bible and Medical Mission were Mrs Mary Jane Kinnaird and her husband Lord Kinnaird, who generously supported the Kinnaird High School for Girls in Lahore. Kinnaird College was founded in 1913 by the Zenana Bible Medical Mission when they started college classes at the Girls' High School.

The Zenana Bible and Medical Mission supported and served ministry among women for many years. In 1957 it became the Bible and Medical Missionary Fellowship. In 1987 it became Interserve, which continues to serve in many nations today, including Pakistan.

Blanche Brenton Carey

Blanche was the daughter of the vicar of Brixham in Devon and a Sunday school teacher. She arrived in Karachi in 1885, serving with the Zenana Bible and Medical Mission. Karachi was a port town with a population of about 70,000. Its people spoke many different languages. Urdu was common but many spoke Marathi, Arabic, Sindhi and Gujarati.

She began to learn Sindhi as soon as she arrived in Karachi so that she could talk to the parents and girls in their own language. There was initial opposition to educating girls from Hindu families, but Blanche set her heart on making a difference.

Blanche in 1942, with her co-worker Minna Ghose

In a career of 65 years in Karachi, she opened nine schools with over 900 students, an orphanage, a teacher training college and a widows' industrial class. She also went on tour to villages, travelling by camel and living very simply. She loved to retell the stories of Jesus in a way that resonated with the women.

Blanche was awarded the *Kaiser-i-Hind* medal in 1928 for her services to the women and girls of India. She celebrated her fiftieth year of service in 1935 but continued to work in her nineties. She died in 1950.

Blanche wrote in 1935: "*I love Sindh and its people. Otherwise, why have I lived here so long and tried to help you and your children in any way I could?*"

The Brenton Carey Hostel for Girls is still open in Karachi.

Minna Ghose

Minna Ghose joined Blanche in 1889 as Principal of the Salt Gate School for Sindhi girls. When the orphanage opened in 1904, Minna Ghose was put in charge of the 14 girls. It later became the Hostel for Girls and the Children's Home.

Minna once asked one of her girls: "*Do you remember what you learned about the Lord Jesus?*" She replied: "*Remember? How can I forget my father and my mother?*"

Chapter 19

1900–1947 : Christian Leaders Who Made a Difference

Sadhu Sundar Singh

Sundar Singh is probably the best known of all Christians born and raised in Punjab. Films have been made of his life and his books in many languages are still read all over the world.

He was born in 1889 into a Sikh family in a village in Patiala District, Punjab. He was brought up in all the traditions of the Sikh religion. His family sent him to the mission school, but he hated the Christian teaching. He even tore up a Bible and burned it. He threw stones at preachers, but still he could not find the peace in his heart.

"Some people become tired at the end of ten minutes or half an hour of prayer. What will they do when they have to spend eternity in the presence of God? We must begin the habit here and become used to being with God."

When he was 14 years old, his mother died. Sundar became very sad and angry. He decided to kill himself by throwing himself under a train. He prayed: *"Oh God, if you do exist, show me the right way, or I will kill myself."* And then one night, he had a vision of a bright light. Jesus Christ was there in the room, with a look of inexpressible joy, peace and love. He heard a voice saying, *"How much longer are you going to search for me? I have come to save you."* Sundar fell on his knees and felt a great peace which he had never felt before. The vision disappeared, but peace and joy stayed within him.

Baptism and commitment

In 1905, on his 16th birthday, he was baptised in Simla. He decided to become a Christian sadhu, so that he could dedicate himself to the Lord.

He travelled with only a Bible in his hand and one blanket and wore the yellow robe of a sadhu or *fakir*. He renounced all worldly pleasures and took up his cross to follow Christ. He owned nothing and never married, convinced that this was the best way to introduce the Gospel to his people. Wherever he went he drew large crowds who came to hear him speak.

Sundar Singh spent one year training at St John's Divinity College in Lahore (see Chapter 13), but he was not a good student. He preferred to travel around the villages of India, the foothills of the Himalayas, to Tibet and Nepal, preaching the Word of God. In Tibet he was thrown into a well for two days, but the Lord miraculously rescued him. He set off for the Himalayas and Tibet in April 1929, and never returned. No news was ever received of him again, but it may be said of him that *"he walked with God and the Lord took him up to Himself"*.

Barkat Ullah: from Karbala to Calvary

"In 1891, on the seventh of the month of Muharram, I was born into a Shi'a Muslim family in a small town called Narowal. Our family was respected by the whole community for its integrity of life, piety and strict observance of religious rites and ceremonies."

That is how Barkat Ullah began the story of his life. His father, Rehmat Ali, was the brother of Ihsan Ullah (see Chapter 14). Barkat was brought up as a pious Muslim, though his father had respect for all religions and regularly read the Bible together with the Qur'an. He sent his son Barkat to study at a Christian school.

One day he was in the bazaar and he saw a missionary, Mr Thomas, preaching the Gospel. Suddenly a big strong man approached the preacher, spat on his face and slapped it. Everyone expected there would be a fight, as Mr Thomas was also big and strong. Barkat wrote afterwards: *"What we saw amazed us. The preacher took out his handkerchief, calmly wiped his face and said: 'God bless you.' Then he continued to preach as if no insult had been offered him."* Barkat Ullah never forgot the experience of watching someone react in a Christian manner.

Shocked, convinced and committed

After leaving the eighth class Barkat Ullah arrived home at the end of the school year. To his amazement he learned that his parents, two sisters and two brothers, had become Christians. His father told him of his 20-year search for truth and that he had finally found it in Christ. Barkat Ullah began to read the New Testament and Christian books by Pfander and Imad-ud-Din (see Chapter 14). He also became convinced, trusted in Christ and was baptised at the age of 16 on 7th July 1907.

A life of Christian service

He gained a Master's degree in Philosophy from Punjab University in 1914 and then taught at Edwardes College in Peshawar and F.C. College. He was ordained as a pastor in 1923 in the Diocese of Lahore. He served as Canon of Lahore Cathedral and Archdeacon of Amritsar in India after partition in 1947. He was elected a Member of the Royal Asiatic Society. He retired in 1956.

"The Cross of Calvary, on which Christ died, became meaningful to me. In that the Lord Jesus had lived and died because of my sins, Himself being sinless, I could see that God had loved me and forgiven my sins, as Christ had loved and forgiven sinners.

I felt that the great burden of sin was lifted off my shoulders. Oh, the joy! The conviction that I had been forgiven brought peace and harmony into my life, and I felt like one flying in the air."

He is best remembered for his many books in Urdu. He wrote especially on the truth of the Bible and to explain his reasons for becoming a Christian. He died in 1971 in New Delhi (India).

Esther John

Esther was born in Madras (now Chennai in India) in 1929. Her family gave her the name Qamar Zia. She was brought up in the Muslim faith, but studied at a Christian school from the age of 17. In school she was impressed by the faithful testimony and behaviour of one of her teachers. She began to study the Bible with growing eagerness. She was so inspired by the book of Isaiah that she quietly converted to Christianity.

In 1947 her family moved to Pakistan. In Karachi she made contact with a missionary, Marian Laugesen, who gave her a New Testament. For a while she worked in an orphanage, and took the name Esther John. Fearing that her family wanted her to marry, she moved north to Sahiwal in Punjab. There she lived and worked in a mission hospital. She stayed with the first Bishop of Karachi, Chandu Ray, and celebrated her first Christmas.

For two years she trained and then became a teacher at the United Bible Training Centre in Gujranwala. She spent the rest of her short life travelling on her bicycle and sharing the Gospel in the villages around Chichawatni. She taught women to read and worked with them in the cotton fields.

On 2nd February 1960 Esther was found murdered on her bed at her home in Chichawatni. She was buried at the Christian cemetery at Sahiwal. A memorial chapel was built in front of the nurses' home in the grounds of the hospital there.

Esther John is one of ten modern martyrs of the twentieth century remembered by statues over the west door of Westminster Abbey in London. She stands alongside nine other Christians who gave their lives for their faith in the twentieth century. The martyrs were unveiled in 1998. The sculptor was Neil Simmons.

The Perfect Way: Why I Became a Follower of al-Maseeh
by Pastor Sultan Mohammad Paul

Sultan was born in Kabul, Afghanistan, in 1881. He moved to India to study Islam. When he was given a Bible, he began to read. *"My object in reading the Bible was to find mistakes in it and to silence Christians in argument."*

But Sultan had many questions about religion. He began to read the Bible and to pray: *"If Christianity is the true religion, then reveal its truth to me. Amen."* Then he found the verse in the Gospel of Matthew where Jesus said: ***"Come to me, all who labour and are heavy-laden, and I will give you rest...."*** He wrote in his book: *"This life-giving verse brought me peace, comfort, and joy and immediately banished all uncertainty from my heart."*

"When I became a Christian, a wonderful change took place in my life. My Muslim friends wondered at it. They marvelled at my mildness, for they knew how easily I used to lose my temper... Sin cannot be removed by repentance alone. It must be cleansed by the sacred blood of our Saviour."

In 1903 he requested baptism. In later life he was ordained as a pastor and became a professor of Arabic at Forman Christian College, Lahore.

Chapter 20

1900–1947 : Some Great Christian Organisations

Much to be thankful for

Today we are thankful for many organisations that give opportunities, training and support to Christian young people. Many of them began before 1947, in the early years of the twentieth century or earlier. After the birth of Pakistan, they have continued to serve the Christian community – and in most cases other communities also. Being run and managed by Christians, they maintain a high standard of excellence and often give special privileges to Christians. Thank God for them.

Gujranwala: The Christian Technical Training Centre

In 1863 the boys' orphanage in Sialkot moved to Gujranwala, overseen by the Presbyterian missionary James Barr and George Scott (see Chapter 10). There was a great famine in 1900 when the harvest failed and many thousands of people were left without food. Many boys arrived in Gujranwala looking for food, and they stayed in the Presbyterian orphanage building.

They were welcomed and taught to speak Punjabi. Then they were given training in weaving, tailoring, shoe making and carpentry. The expenses were covered by gifts received for the Great Famine. It was the start of the Boys' Industrial Home and Technical School. The first director of the school was the Rev. Osborne Crowe.

By 1903 150 boys were living in the hostels and getting technical training. With the arrival of the motor car, the school faced a new problem. Who was qualified to repair this new machine? God had an answer. In 1925 Mr F.A. Whitfield

arrived in Gujranwala. He was *"a trained mechanic, from airplanes to locomotives"*. He organised a motor and machine department.

The centre continued to grow and develop. By 1961 thousands of young men had received training and skills that enabled them to get good jobs. In that year a large building was erected. In 1970 it was given a new name: The Christian

Technical Training Centre (CTTC). Through outstanding leadership and staff, it has served the Christian community with quality and professionalism. Courses are given in electrical technology, architecture, computing and more.

The Bible Society

Bible work in Punjab began in 1809, one year after the formation of the Bible Society of India, Burma and Ceylon. There was, however, no Bible available in Urdu until Henry Martyn's New Testament was printed in Calcutta in 1817 (see Chapter 7). The first complete Urdu Bible was published in 1843.

In 1862 a large group of Protestant missionaries – known as the General Council of Indian Missionaries – met in Lahore. They discussed and decided that there was an urgent need to open an office to promote the printing and distribution of the Bible across Punjab.

Finally, in January 1863 the efforts of the General Council were successful. The British & Foreign Bible Society opened the Punjab office at the present site in Anarkali, Lahore. At that time the population of Punjab was estimated to be 15 million, of which fewer than 80,000 could read.

In 1947 the name of the Punjab Auxiliary was changed to Pakistan Bible Society. It was registered as a Society in 1956 and in 1967 became a full member of the United Bible Societies (UBS). This is an organisation that connects national Bible Societies into a worldwide fellowship in 146 countries.

"The mission of the Pakistan Bible Society is to make the Holy Bible available in the language people speak in a format that is creative, easy to understand, and affordable to ordinary people, so that all can experience its life-changing message."

Celebrating the Bible Society in 2013

In February 2013, the Pakistan Bible Society celebrated 150 years since its birth. The General Pakistan Post issued a special postage stamp, printed by Pakistan Security Printing Corporation, Karachi,

to celebrate *"150 years of faithful services of the Pakistan Bible Society"*.

The Bible Society in Lahore also opened a Bible museum to commemorate its history promoting the reading of the Bible.

More than 400 items are on display in the museum together with hundreds of books that teach the story of Christianity in India and Pakistan. There is also a copy of the first edition of the Urdu translation of the Bible.

The curse of leprosy

Leprosy is referred to 68 times in the Bible. What the Bible calls leprosy probably covered several diseases that affected the skin and might include diseases other than what we know as leprosy today. Nevertheless, it was viewed as a curse from God, and lepers were thrown out of society because of the fear of catching the disease. Jesus healed several lepers.

The disease of leprosy that we know today damages nerves close to the surface of the skin. The first signs are often coloured patches on the body that have lost any feeling. If not treated, the nerve damage spreads. Without any feelings in their hands and feet, people with leprosy can hurt themselves, which can quickly lead to infection and permanent disability. Leprosy can cause muscle paralysis, resulting in clawed fingers and foot drop. This makes it difficult for people to walk or use their hands.

The Leprosy Mission in Pakistan

Wellesley Bailey arrived in India as a missionary in 1869. He was sent to teach in a school in Ambala in Punjab. One day he was invited to visit a colony of lepers. He was shocked by what he saw. Many had clawed hands, some were blind, and some had disfigured faces. *"I felt that if there was ever a Christ-like work in the world it was to go amongst these poor sufferers and bring them the Gospel."* Wellesley returned home to Ireland and in 1878 he and his wife Alice founded the Leprosy Mission.

The British Leprosy Mission opened the Rawalpindi Leprosy Hospital in 1904. Dr R.R. Stewart, a teacher in Gordon College, was so moved by the sight of a colony of lepers that he dedicated himself to open a hospital. Lepers from all over British India used to come to this hospital for treatment.

In 1968 the German Leprosy Relief Association took over the Rawalpindi Leprosy Hospital. It has 40 beds and the clinic is open every day. A thousand new leprosy cases are discovered every year in Pakistan.

Dr Ruth Pfau and the Marie Adelaide Hospital, Karachi

Ruth Pfau was born in Germany in 1929. Her life was changed when, as a student, she met a Dutch Christian who had suffered terribly but was committed to preach *"love and forgiveness"*. Ruth arrived in Pakistan in 1960 with the Catholic order, the Daughters of the Heart of Mary. She dedicated the next 57 years to care for leprosy suffers in the Marie Adelaide Leprosy Centre in Karachi. She died in 2017 and was given a state funeral in honour of her service to the poor.

The Punjab Religious Book Society (PRBS)

Preachers and evangelists across Punjab enjoyed great freedom to preach the Gospel in the twentieth century. Many would go into the streets and villages, both missionaries and local evangelists, and begin to preach. A crowd always gathered to listen. And then the preacher would give an invitation, and offer to give away leaflets and booklets about the Gospel message. The Bible Society printed Bibles, but there was clearly a need for more literature to be written and printed.

When the Bible Society opened its offices in Anarkali, Lahore, in 1863, it also opened a Christian publishing house next door. This was the beginning of the Punjab Religious Book Society (PRBS). It began to publish, print and sell Christian booklets and tracts.

Mr H.E. Perkins was Assistant Commissioner of Amritsar and Rawalpindi. In 1886 he left his Government job and joined the Church Missionary Society. He became the Editorial Secretary and Chairman of the Punjab Bible and Religious Book Society. It was said that *"he greatly helped forward the preparation, publication, and circulation of books in Punjabi and Urdu".*

PRBS served the growing Christian community for more than 100 years, providing Gospel booklets that explained the Christian faith for evangelism. Sadly, after serving the church faithfully for many years, PRBS is now closed, but many others have taken over the task of printing books for the church.

Nirali Kitaben, MIK (Masihi Isha'at Khana) and the Daughters of St Paul now serve the church in Pakistan. We tell their story in Chapter 24. But the first publisher of quality Christian literature in Punjab was the PRBS.

Punjab Religious Book Society tracts and booklets

These are some of the booklets printed and sold by the PRBS in 1904 and 1905. The sale of books increased steadily. The records tell that by 1904 PRBS had published more than 1,000 booklets and tracts. They also employed colporteurs – evangelists who went into the streets to sell books and give out tracts.

Part 6

(Chapters 21 to 30)

From
the Birth of Pakistan (1947)
to
the Present Day

14th August: Pakistan's Independence Day

Chapter 21

1947 : Christians and Pakistan's Independence

14th August 1947

Pakistanis all over the world look back to 1947 as the year in which their nation gained independence from foreign rule. It was a day of hope and joy, when all communities could take pride in what had been achieved, and look forward with excitement to a new day of freedom and prosperity. On 11th August Mr Muhammad Ali Jinnah (the *Quaid-e-Azam*) announced:

"You are free; you are free to go to your temples, you are free to go to your mosques or to any other place of worship in this State of Pakistan. You may belong to any religion or caste or creed that has nothing to do with the business of the State."

"My guiding principle will be justice and complete impartiality, and I am sure that with your support and co-operation, I can look forward to Pakistan becoming one of the greatest nations of the world."

The path to Independence

The All-India Muslim League was a political party established in Dhaka (now the capital of Bangladesh) in 1906. Its aim was to stand up for the rights of Muslims across India. Mohammed Ali Jinnah, who was born in 1876 in Karachi and trained as a lawyer in London, joined and became leader of the Muslim League in 1913. But it was not until much later that he began to dream of an independent homeland for the Muslims of India.

On 29th December 1930 Sir Muhammad Iqbal gave his presidential address to the All-India Muslim League annual session. He said:

"I would like to see the Punjab, North-West Frontier Province, Sindh and Baluchistan amalgamated into a single State.
Self-government ... appears to me to be the final destiny of the Muslims, at least of North-West India."

From the beginning of the independence movement, many Christians supported Mr Jinnah and his dream of freedom. When Jinnah launched the *DAWN* newspaper in October 1941 to give publicity for the All-India Muslim League, he appointed a Christian, Pothan Joseph, as its first editor.

Mr Elmer Chaudhry, a devout Roman Catholic, was a Science and Urdu teacher in St Anthony's High School for 15 years (and father of squadron leader Cecil Chaudhry). He used his camera to take some of the most famous historical photos of the Pakistan Movement. When Jinnah came to Lahore in February 1936 Chaudhry took his picture, which he considered a great honour. He joined the *Pakistan Times* as a staff reporter in 1949 and was awarded the *Sitara-i-Imtiaz* by the Pakistan Government for his outstanding contribution to Pakistan. He died on his 104th birthday in 2013.

Joshua Fazl-Ud-Din

Joshua Fazal-Ud-Din, born in 1903, gained his degree at F.C. College, Lahore, and passed his law exams in 1933. He wrote newspaper articles to promote Jinnah's vision. His support of a separate homeland won the heart of Choudhry Rahmat Ali when many Muslim leaders were thinking that it was impossible. He said *"it was in accordance with the voice of God"*.

However, he is best known as a great Christian writer. He wrote a book on *The Future of Christians in Pakistan*. He also wrote the life of Christ in Punjabi verse. After Independence, he was an elected Member of the Punjab Legislative Assembly and Deputy Law Minister of West Pakistan. He died in 1973.

S.P. Singha and the birth of Pakistan

In June 1947 the British Government appointed a lawyer, Sir Cyril Radcliffe, to draw the borders for the new nations of Pakistan and India. His aim was to leave as many Sikhs and Hindus in India and Muslims in Pakistan as possible. He was given only five weeks to complete the job.

Dewan Bahadur Satya Prakash Singha was a well-known Christian leader in Punjab. He was born in Pasrur in 1893. As Registrar of Punjab University he introduced the Matriculation exam system and was awarded the *Dewan Bahadur* medal by the British Government.

Singha was elected to the Punjab Assembly in 1937. As a Christian he became a strong supporter of the Pakistan Movement. In a famous speech he said, *"At the time of partition of the sub-continent of India, in the entire country, the Christians should be counted with Muslims."* In November 1946 Singha said: *"From today Jinnah is our leader..."* He worked tirelessly to convince the Christians to become part of Pakistan.

On 23rd June 1947, two months before Independence, a meeting was held at the Punjab Legislative Assembly to determine whether West Punjab should be a part of Pakistan or not. S.P. Singha, as Speaker of the Assembly, cast his vote in favour of Pakistan. The other Christian members of the assembly, Fazal Elahi and Cecil Gibbon, followed him. Pakistan won by three votes and West Punjab was included in Pakistan. S.P. Singha sadly died in 1948.

C.E. Gibbons, from the Anglo Indian Community, became Deputy Speaker of the National Assembly in 1955. Chaudhry Chandu Lal, a member of the Muslim League's Executive and also a Christian, was a Pakistani lawyer who served as the Deputy Speaker of the second Provincial Assembly of the Punjab between 1955 and 1955.

Honoured by the Pakistan Post Office

In April 2016 the Pakistan Post Office issued a special 10 rupee postage stamp, *"Recognising the services for Pakistan of Dewan Bahadur S.P. Singha"*. This was a great honour for Pakistan's Christians.

Christians in the new State of Pakistan

The partition of Punjab in 1947 led to huge chaos. Many millions of Hindus and Sikhs living in West Punjab left their homes and travelled east into India – and many millions of Muslims in India moved towards Pakistan. Over 12 million people were uprooted from their homeland and travelled on foot, bullock carts and trains to their promised new home. About a million people died.

In the chaos most Christians stayed where they were, as they were not the target of violence. Instead, Christians ministered to the wounded, sick and needy of all religious communities, often at risk to their lives. They painted crosses on their homes and sewed crosses on their clothes. The sign of the cross often saved them from being killed by the violent mob.

By 1947, there were more than 500,000 Christians in Pakistan, both from Punjabi low-caste, Muslim and other backgrounds. The majority of Christians in Karachi were from Goan Catholic, Tamil, North Indian and Anglo-Indian families. In recent years numbers of Marwari and other tribal groups have also turned to Christ in Sindh. Since Independence, the church has become increasingly diverse in both origin and culture.

Ghulam Masih Naaman: Freedom Fighter

Ghulam Naaman was born in a Muslim family in Jammu and Kashmir in 1930, but his home town was Zafarwal in Sialkot.

India was in turmoil as Independence drew near. Naaman said: *"My desire was to please God. I was led by my religious leaders to join the freedom fighter forces to liberate Kashmir from the Hindus."* He joined the fighters who were burning Hindu villages in Kashmir.

Naaman had met Christians before and his conscience was troubled. He was about to kill a small Christian girl in Kashmir when she said: *"The Lord Jesus is here to save and protect us."* He was terrified and could not kill her. *"I knew that I could not go on with my present life. I no longer felt that I was pleasing Allah by killing infidels. After returning to my quarters, I could not sleep. The name of Jesus Christ kept ringing in my ears."*

He knew that he must pray to God. *"I was searching and praying in deep darkness. I prayed to God to put me on the right path. God answered. 'My grace is sufficient for you.' These words rang in my ears. He forgave all the evil I had committed. I was a new person, that night of 5th May 1949."*

Ghulam Masih Naaman became a much-loved pastor in Sukkur. He died in November 1997.

The first India-Pakistan War: 1947–1949

Sadly India and Pakistan went to war on 22nd October 1947. The population of Kashmir was 4 million, most of them Muslims. It was expected that they would join the new State of Pakistan, but the ruler of Jammu and Kashmir was a Hindu. He wanted to join India. This was the cause of the war that continued until a United Nations Commission arranged a cease-fire on 1st January 1949. Kashmir was divided with the agreement that the Kashmiris would hold a referendum to decide their future. This never took place. Kashmir remains an area of disagreement and conflict.

Many Pakistani Christians have served the country with honour and distinction in the Army, Navy and Airforce. In 1948 Flight Lieutenant Alfred Jagjivan was caught in conflict with an Indian fighter pilot. It was reported that Jagjivan shouted: *"Do not give in! We will live for Pakistan and die for Pakistan."*

Samuel Martin Burke

Samuel Martin Burke was born in 1906 in Martinpur. His father, Janab Khairudin, a school headmaster, was the first high school graduate from the village. He was a poet and used the name *Barq* (meaning *lightning* in Urdu) when he wrote poems. Samuel took this as his name – Burke.

Samuel was a brilliant student and won a scholarship to Government College, Lahore, to study science to become a doctor. Then he changed his mind and studied history, philosophy, Persian and Urdu. He served as Assistant Commissioner in the Indian Civil Service, and in 1941 became a district and sessions judge. At Independence in 1947 he retired to Martinpur.

With partition and the creation of Pakistan in 1947, Burke assisted Sir Muhammad Zafrullah Khan in setting up the new country's fledgling Foreign Ministry and went on to serve as a diplomat in 11 countries. His first posting was as a counsellor at the High Commission in London – a Christian in charge of one of the most important tasks of the Foreign Service. He went on to become Pakistan's ambassador to Thailand and finally as the High Commissioner to Canada between 1959 and 1961.

He finally quit in 1961 and retired to write books and lecture in the United States. He died at the age of 104 in 2010.

Chapter 22

The Growth of Churches Across Pakistan

The amazing increase of Christian believers

St Peter's Church in Karachi opened a new building in 2011 to accommodate about 5,000 worshippers.

Since the birth of Pakistan, Christian churches have grown and increased everywhere. Missionaries were still welcomed by the Government of Pakistan. Their contribution was greatly valued by the new State, especially in the areas of education, medicine and health care, and technical skills.

However, Pakistani leaders increasingly took control in almost every area of Christian ministry. And as national leadership grew and matured, so the need for foreign help declined and the Government was less willing to provide visas for missionaries. Today very few foreign missionaries are still in leadership in Pakistan.

The result has been both good and bad. The church across Pakistan now stands strong with good, wise and spiritual leaders. At the same time there has been a sad increase in religious politics, corruption and conflict within the church.

Pakistan
How many people?
How many Christians?

When Pakistan was born in 1947, there were two parts:

- East Pakistan, made up mostly of Bengali-speaking Muslims (86%) and Hindus (13%). East Pakistan became Bangladesh in 1971.

- West Pakistan (Punjab, Sindh, Baluchistan and the North-West Frontier).

This is the population figure for West Pakistan and (since 1971) Pakistan.

1951
34 million (33,740,000)

1961
43million (42,880,000)

1972
65 million (65,309,000)

1981
84 million (84,254,000)

1998
132 million (132,352,279)

2017
208 million (207,774,520)

The number of Christians has also grown. According to the Government statistics, there were 2,642,048 (1.27%) Christians in 2017. Many believe there are actually many more, possibly as many as 5 or 6 million.

The main churches

The Roman Catholic Church

When Pakistan gained Independence, the Catholic Union of India granted independence to its branches in Sindh and Baluchistan in October 1947. Joseph Cordeiro, Archbishop of Karachi, became the first Pakistani cardinal, elevated to the position by Pope Paul VI on 5th March 1973.

The Roman Catholic Church in Pakistan continued to grow, and today about half of Pakistan's Christians are Roman Catholics. The Church is active in education, health and other social aspects of daily life in addition to its spiritual work.

The Church of Pakistan

In 1929 several churches in North India (including Punjab and Sindh) began to discuss joining together as one Church. In 1965 a Plan for Church Union was agreed. On 1st November 1970, in Lahore Cathedral, four Pakistani churches became one. And so the Church of Pakistan came into being.

The total membership of the united Church was 200,000. As three of the uniting churches already had bishops in place, they continued as bishops of the Church of Pakistan.

The united Church now has eight dioceses, and the bishops elect a moderator to provide overall leadership. The Church of Pakistan is a member of the World Council of Churches.

> **The churches that joined to become the Church of Pakistan**
>
> - **The Anglican Church (CMS)**
> - **The Church of Scotland**
> - **The Methodist Church**
> - **The Lutheran Church**
>
>  **World Council of Churches**

The Presbyterian Church of Pakistan

The Presbyterian Church of Pakistan grew from the work of early missionaries: Charles Forman, Andrew Gordon and many others. Through missionaries and many national pastors, the Presbyterian Church grew to be one of the largest Protestant denominations.

Pakistan

Sadly, however, many divisions and conflicts have divided the Presbyterian churches. They are led by a synod (an assembly of elected leaders), and there has often been division in the Church over leadership, authority and the control of property. In 1968 a major division occurred in the Presbyterian Church in Pakistan. About a third of the members divided over leadership in the Church. In recent years much of the division has been healed and the churches continue to grow and bless their people.

The Pentecostal churches

In 1940 a Pentecostal pastor from South India, Pastor M. K. Chacko, began to visit Lahore to hold worship services and to give Pentecostal teaching. He invited another South Indian Pentecostal pastor, Pastor K.J. Samuel and his wife Mariamma to join him to provide regular pastoral care for the Pentecostal church. Special meetings were regularly arranged in Forman Christian College.

Pastor Samuel led worship services at F.C. College in the home of Dr E.J. Sinclair. Dr Sinclair had been a student in the college, then a teacher and was finally appointed as Principal until his retirement in 1968. He was baptised in the Holy Spirit during a prayer meeting led by Robert Cummings, a Presbyterian missionary.

There are several Pentecostal churches in Pakistan, known as the Assemblies of God, the Philadelphia Pentecostal Church and others. The largest of the Pentecostal churches is the Full Gospel Assemblies.

Full Gospel Assemblies of Pakistan

In 1943 Karen Kometh, a lady missionary of the Scandinavian Free Mission, arrived in Lahore. The Full Gospel Assemblies began with one church in 1947. In the early days of the FGA church movement, missionaries from Sweden gave great support.

Now FGA has 300 churches all over the country. In total there are more than 100,000 adult members in their churches. A Bible Correspondence School was established in 1970 that has reached millions of people, and Sunday school ministry began in 1972. A Christian monthly magazine was launched in 1985.The FGA Education Project oversees 25 schools that provide Christian schooling at little cost to more than 2,000 Christian children.

Bakht Singh and the Brethren churches

Bakht Singh Chabra was born to Sikh parents near Sargodha in 1903. He studied at a mission high school and graduated from Punjab University. He then travelled to England and Canada for further studies. He later wrote: *"We hated Christians, and we used to make fun of Bible teachers and pastors."* But in Canada he studied the Bible and came to personal faith in Christ. He was baptised in 1932 and returned to India. He started

preaching the Gospel in the streets of Karachi, and in the villages in Sindh and in Quetta. He testified: *"Can I live without breathing? When Christ is my life how can I live without Him?"* In 1937 he took meetings in Youngsonabad and Martinpur, and many people were saved (see Chapter 16). It was the beginning of the Brethren movement in Pakistan.

Brethren churches began to form about two hundred years ago in Ireland. Today they have an estimated 26,000 assemblies worldwide. In Pakistan there are several

Brethren Church baptism for believers

branches of Brethren with several thousand committed believers. Some have pastors, others are led by elders. They believe that the Bible is the first authority in matters of faith and practice. They only baptise those who confess personal faith in Christ.

There are several different branches of the Brethren Church in Pakistan, The publishing house MIK is run by the Brethren Church, and the Bible Training Centre in Lahore. Several Brethren churches also run schools for Christians.

Seventh-day Adventist Church

Dr V.L. Mann started work for the Seventh-day Adventist Church in Gujranwala in 1913. In 1916 they bought land in Chuharkana (Farooqabad) near Sheikhupura, which became the centre of their work.

The Pakistan Adventist Seminary and College (PASC) developed from a small boys' school founded in 1920. The Church grew slowly, as they focused on issues of health. They also issued a study course which helped many people to understand the Bible better. The Church numbers several thousand members.

The Church has certain distinctive beliefs, such as worshipping on Saturday, which is the Sabbath or seventh day, rather than Sunday.

The Seventh-day Adventist Hospital in Karachi was built in 1950. In 1959 a new wing was added, so that it is now able to care for 110 patients.

Many other churches
and hundreds of independent groups of Christians

In Pakistan today there are many other church denominations – the Baptist Bible Fellowship and the Indus Christian Fellowship (ICF) in Sindh, the Association of Evangelical Churches of Pakistan (AEC), the Associate Reformed Presbyterians (ARP) and more.

However, probably the largest groups of churches across Pakistan are small independent meetings of Christians, often led by a pastor or local leader, gathered together to worship Christ in prayer and song, and to study the Bible. Some meeting in private homes, or in the open air under a tree. No one has counted how many such groups there are, but probably hundreds, maybe thousands.

Chapter 23

Pakistani Christians in National Leadership

Outstanding Pakistani leaders

Throughout the twentieth century, and especially in the years since Pakistan's Independence, Pakistani Christians have taken important leadership at every level in society. Gifted Pakistanis have shown ability in business, especially in banking and insurance. In the Army, Airforce and Navy, Pakistani Christians have demonstrated bravery and loyalty. There have been many inspiring Christian leaders in education, medicine and politics. In this chapter we can only highlight a few.

Group Captain Cecil Chaudhry

Cecil Chaudhry was born on 27th August 1941 to the only Christian (Roman Catholic) family of the village Dalwal in the Salt Range of Punjab.

His father, Elmer Chaudhry, was a well-known photographer and teacher (see Chapter 21). Cecil studied at St Anthony's School in Lahore, and gained his BSc in Physics at F.C. College. He married Iris in 1964.

Cecil and Iris Chaudhry

"By faith I'm a Christian but my religion is humanity."

He joined the Air Force Academy in 1958 where he studied aeronautics and mechanical engineering. He became a pilot in the Pakistan Air Force after his graduation from the PAF Academy.

Cecil became a national hero in the 1965 and 1971 wars with India. As a fighter pilot he showed great courage and success in air battles with the Indian Air Force. In the 1971 war his plane was hit over Indian territory. His plane crashed but he returned safely to Pakistan.

For his bravery and service he was awarded the *Sitara-e-Jurat (Star of Courage)* and the *Sitara-e-Basalat (Star of Good Conduct)*.

After leaving the Air Force he served as Principal of St Anthony's School for 14 years, before becoming Principal of Saint Mary's Academy in Rawalpindi. He retired in July 2011.

Both Cecil and Iris were active in working for human rights, especially to improve the lives of disabled children. Cecil Chaudhry died in Lahore in 2012. He was buried with full military honours at the Jail Road Christian Cemetery.

Flight Lieutenant Cecil Chaudhry, Wing Commander Muhammad Anwar Shamim and Flight Lieutenant Imtiaz Bhatti with an F-86 Sabre photographed during 1965 war.

Christian leaders in public life

Eric Gordon Hall was born in Rangoon, Burma (now Myanmar) in 1922, but his family migrated to British India in 1942 and settled in Lahore. He joined the Pakistan Air Force and saw action in the 1965 war, one of the most distinguished pilots belonging to the Christian minority.

After the war he served as the Vice Chief of Air Staff and also Director-General of the Pakistan Air Force's Science Research Laboratories (AFSRL), where he led atomic weapons research efforts as part of Pakistan's nuclear technology project. He was given an honourable discharge from the Air Force and made Director General of the Civil Aviation Authority (CAA) for the Government of Pakistan. He died in the USA in 1998.

Leslie Norman Mungavin (known to his friends as Jack) was born in 1923 and joined the Royal Indian Navy in 1945. At partition in 1947 he transferred to the Pakistan Navy. His career gradually progressed till his retirement as Deputy Chief of Naval Staff at the rank of Rear Admiral. During his 33 years of service with the Pakistan Navy, Mungavin held a number of command appointments at sea and ashore at Naval Headquarters. He served on various Pakistan Navy ships and was acknowledged as a leading navigation specialist. He was taken prisoner in Chittagong during the 1971 war with India. After his return to Pakistan he served as the Chairman of the Board of the Pakistan National Shipping Corporation. He died in 1995 and the Pakistan Navy honoured him with a full military funeral.

Major General Julian Peter also fought with distinction in the war in East Pakistan. He was the first Christian elevated to the position of Major General in April 1993.

Many other Christians have risen to prominence in the Pakistani Army, Navy, Airforce and civil services. Space forbids us to mention them all.

Mrs Aasiya Nasir

Aasiya Nasir is a Christian politician who was a member of the National Assembly of Pakistan. She was elected on reserved Christian seats in 2002 and re-elected in 2013 as a candidate of Jamiat Ulema-e-Islam.

Aasiya was born in 1971 in Quetta and gained her Master's degree in English Literature from Government Girls' College. She showed great courage when she delivered a speech in the National Assembly after the assassination of Shahbaz Bhatti in 2011. Pointing towards the portrait of Jinnah she cried: *"Where is your Pakistan?"*

> *"Encouraging women in all fields of life including politics is a need of the time. If women consist of 50% of the population then they should advance in all spheres of life. Our youth can change the fate of the country."*

Mrs Tara Joy James

Tara James was born in Sargodha in 1931. Her father was the son of Archdeacon Ihsan Ullah (see Chapter 14) and her uncle was Pastor Barkat Ullah (see Chapter 19).

Tara graduated from Kinnaird College in 1959 and did a Master's degree in English Literature from Karachi. She received the Gold Medal as best student of the university. In 1948 she married Banner James, who was working with Burmah Shell in Karachi.

She began her teaching career in 1961 in the Convent of Jesus and Mary in Lahore. Then moving to Karachi she taught in Our Lady of Fatima, and in 1969 became Principal of the Trinity Methodist Girls' High School.

God then called her into full-time Christian work. She left her well-paid Government post and joined the Pakistan Fellowship of Evangelical Students (PFES) in 1973. God used her to bring many students, especially girls, to Christ.

She became "Auntie Tara" – a much-loved spiritual auntie to hundreds of Christian students. She died on Easter Monday 2001.

"I can pray for people and I want to pray for people.
I feel that is my special ministry now."

Dr Mira Phailbus

Mira Phailbus was Principal of Kinnaird College for Women in Lahore for 32 years. During her years at Kinnaird the college was granted university status. It was said that *"with a faith that moves mountains, she turned the college into a centre of excellence"*.

Dr Phailbus also served as Minister for Education and Minority Affairs in the Punjab Government. She became the first woman in Pakistan to be appointed as the Government "Ombudsman", an important job to deal with people's complaints and protect their rights.

She is recognised internationally for her great contribution to education in Pakistan, especially for women and girls.

Chief Justice Alvin Robert Cornelius

Alvin Cornelius was born in Agra in British India in 1903. His family were Roman Catholics. He joined the Indian Civil Service and was appointed Assistant Commissioner in Punjab. He began his judicial career in 1943 in the Lahore High Court, where he was appointed Associate Judge.

Cornelius decided to remain in Pakistan and became an important figure in the country's legal history. He served as the law secretary and adviser to Law Minister Jogendra Nath Mandal and Prime Minister Liaquat Ali Khan.

Cornelius was regarded as a man of justice. He fought against religious extremism. As a Christian, he warned against *"despair and a common readiness to anticipate the worst"*. In 1960, President Ayub Khan nominated him to the position of Chief Justice of Pakistan. He became one of the most famous and influential figures ever to serve on the

Supreme Court. He continued to work for the protection of the rights of minorities and freedom of religious practices.

Cornelius and his wife, Ione Francis, lived very simply in two rooms at Faletti's Hotel in Lahore. When Ione died in November 1989, after a marriage of 58 years, he moved into a single room. He never moved to the official house of the Chief Justice. Cornelius died in 1991.

GEO News reported: March 2013
"Street sweeper's son Labha Masih becomes judge in Punjab"

Zeshan Labha Masih, whose parents swept the streets and bazaars of Okara to earn their livelihood, became a judge in 2013 after having passed the Punjab Public Service Commission exam.

His successful appointment spread a wave of happiness and joy in his community. *"He has worked day and night for this. He barely had time for himself or the family but now all his hard work has paid off,"* said his wife, Arzoo Masih. Zeshan, who was next promoted to Assistant Commissioner, is now a role model for those who dream of greater ambition for their lives.

"I am totally opposed to those who say that Pakistan is an impossible place for Christians. We need to make up our minds: 'Yes, I can do it!' Of course there are problems, but not enough to stop someone who is determined. If you have the urge to succeed, you will definitely succeed."

"I am an optimist. Our community has a bright future. Today young people are beginning to realise the importance of education. This will transform our society."

Too many to mention

Space does not allow us to acknowledge the huge contribution of Christians who have lived and served Pakistan since Independence.

Kamran Michael was born on 9th October 1973 in Lahore. He graduated in 1995 from the University of the Punjab. He worked in business before being elected as Member of the Punjab Provincial Assembly in 2002. He became Federal Minister for Ports and Shipping in the Government of Nawaz Sharif.

Stephen Raymond began his time at St Patrick's School, Karachi, as a maths teacher, and later Principal in 1985. He oversaw the education of numerous Muslim young men who went on to become national leaders. He loved to quote Mother Teresa, saying to students and faculty alike, "Do small things with great love." This is something that he lived out each and every day.

Dr E.J. Sinclair, a local Christian, served Forman Christian College for over 50 years as a faculty member and then as Principal. Sinclair Hall in the college is named in his honour. President Musharraf used to say he was the single most important influence in his life.

Pakistani Christians on the world stage:

Dr James Shera

Dr James Shera made history in 1988 when he became the first Pakistani to be elected Mayor of Rugby. Born in the village of Lohianwala in Gujranwala in 1946, James won a scholarship to study at the Catholic University of Louvain in Belgium. He hitch-hiked to Italy, where he caught a train to Brussels to start his studies.

He came to England in 1970 and took a job at Rugby station as a railway guard. As Mayor of Rugby he was awarded the MBE in 2007, and the Pakistani award of *Hilal-e-Quaid Azam* in 2023, and *Sitara-e-Pakistan* (Star of Pakistan), awarded by the President of Pakistan for services to the community and interfaith relations. He has achieved so much for Pakistani Christians.

Mgr Michael Nazir Ali

Michael Nazir-Ali was born in Karachi in 1949. His father's family were Shi'a Muslims and his mother was from a Christian background but from the Muslim university town of Aligarh in North India. He studied Islamic history and economics in St Patrick's College and Karachi University. He formally joined the Church of Pakistan at the age of 20.

Michael had an outstanding academic career, studying theology at Oxford, Cambridge and Harvard universities. He was ordained as an Anglican priest in 1976 in Pakistan. He moved to Lahore with his family, became Bishop of Raiwind in 1984 – at the time the youngest bishop in the Anglican Communion.

When he moved to England in 1986 he worked with the Archbishop of Canterbury, served as General Secretary of the Church Mission Society for five years and then became Bishop of Rochester. This gave him great influence in the media as well as in the House of Lords where he was a member for 15 years.

In 2021 he was received into the Catholic Church where he is now a Priest of the Ordinariate of Our Lady of Walsingham and Prelate of Honour to His Holiness Pope Francis. He now also teaches at the Angelicum in Rome.

Michael summarised his dream for his fellow citizens:

"In the end, what we need in Pakistan is a change in mind-set which recognises all citizens as equal, with equal responsibilities and rights. Christians need to emerge from their ghettoes to take their rightful place in society and to continue working for the wellbeing of all their fellow citizens. The future of Christians in Pakistan depends on whether the country chooses to follow the path of its founders or to follow those who opposed its creation and now wish to turn it into a theocratic state where only one kind of narrative is allowed to prevail."

Chapter 24

The Great Christian Ministries

The increase of Christian ministries across Pakistan

The growing Christian community in Pakistan is divided into thousands of churches. Some have large and beautiful buildings, others worship in small halls or homes or even in the open air. No one has counted the number of churches in Pakistan, but it is certainly several thousand. Alongside the churches there are organisations that are often called "parachurch" organisations. They serve the church with various special ministries, such as books, films, Sunday school materials, training conferences, evangelism programmes, and other services. We have already looked at some that began long ago (see Chapter 20). Many more have begun since Pakistan became independent.

Pakistan Fellowship of Evangelical Students (PFES)

In 1956 a young man with a vision, Gordon Olson, came to Pakistan with the Brethren Assemblies to work among university students in Lahore. He planned to establish Christian student groups in universities and  colleges. When he left, he handed over leadership to Maqbool Gill. In August 1969 a few friends met together in Murree and they gave their ministry a name: The Pakistan Fellowship of Evangelical Students.

In 1970 Mr B. U. Khokhar joined the staff and later became the first National General Secretary. He worked closely with Mrs Tara James. In 1980 Irfan Jamil took over as General Secretary and the work was expanded to the main cities of the country. For many years Mrs Tara James (see Chapter 23) was a valuable staff member, loved by many for her teaching and friendship.

PFES is an active fellowship of committed Christians, involved in evangelism among students, helping Christian students to grow in their faith through Bible study and prayer, and to develop a biblical world view.

Campus Crusade and the *Jesus Film*

In 1951 an American couple, Bill and his wife Vonette Bright, dedicated their lives to spreading the Gospel. They founded the movement known as Campus Crusade for Christ, which now works in 191 countries, including Pakistan. In 1959 Kundan Massey started the ministry of Campus Crusade in Sialkot, Lahore and then Karachi.

One of the most effective of their many ministries has been the *Jesus Film*, which has been translated into more than 1,000 languages, including Urdu and Punjabi. Millions of people have watched the wonderful story of Jesus, His life, death and resurrection.

Scripture Union

In 1901 an English missionary Mr R.D. Archibald laid the foundation of Scripture Union in India. He trained Rev. Paul Das who was given charge of North India. After the birth of Pakistan in 1947, Mr Cecil Johnston continued the work based in Lahore. Rev. Sadiq B. Mall was the first Pakistani to join SU Pakistan in 1953. He worked faithfully, and the Lord blessed the ministry.

Scripture Union visits schools to form Bible study groups for students, holds summer camps and produces daily Bible notes to encourage regular Bible reading.

Masihi Isha'at Khana (MIK)

Dennis Clark arrived in Bombay as an airforce pilot in 1941. He married Gladys in Delhi and together they moved to Lahore. They worked with the Brethren Assemblies and began a local Urdu speaking congregation called *Bethany*. When they moved on to Peshawar in 1943 that little assembly continued to grow and plant other congregations.

In 1946 he met Brother Bakht Singh in Madras. Together they discussed the need for books to teach the Gospel and establish Christians in their faith. Dennis returned to Lahore and founded a Christian publishing house, called Masihi Isha'at Khana (Christian Publishing House). Land

was bought at 36 Ferozepur Road and a printing press obtained. Six years later Dennis moved to Delhi and founded a similar ministry there (MSS).

MIK continues to publish high-quality Christian books, mostly in Urdu, to serve the church. One of their greatest publications was the Bible Dictionary and the Bible Concordance, among many other titles.

The Pakistan Bible Correspondence School

The Pakistan Bible Correspondence School (PBCS) was established by a group of missionaries and Christian leaders in 1957. They had the vision to reach out all over Pakistan to make the Word of God available through Bible study courses that could be studied at home. Centres were opened in five areas: Faisalabad, Karachi, Shikarpur, Dera Ismail Khan and Rawalpindi.

According to their own reports, from 1957 to 2022, 685,000 people had studied the courses and received certificates and New Testaments. That means that almost a million Pakistanis had studied the Word of God. They have 25 courses in Urdu and Sindhi and more than 50 in English.

Nirali Kitaben

The Adult Basic Education Society (ABES) was founded by Presbyterian missionary Ed Carlson in 1971. Ed then passed the leadership of ABES to Vincent David and founded Nirali Kitaben as part of its adult literacy programme.

Nirali KItaben, under the leadership of David Diwan, publishes adult literacy and public health books, but their best-selling title is the *Sialkot Convention Songbook*. Nirali Kitaben also publishes Bible curriculum books for Christian schools.

Evangelical Literature Service (ELS), Karachi

Miles and Beryl Sim came from Canada in 1961 to open a bookshop in their home in Tariq Road, which later moved to the Salvation Army centre in Saddar. They have also published a few Christian books, and the shop is still open for business.

Daughters of St Paul Bookshops

The Daughters of St Paul run five bookshops in Lahore, Rawalpindi, Faisalabad, Multan and Karachi. They are Roman Catholic publishers and the main distributors of Bibles, First Holy Communion books, Mass vestments, rosaries and Christian CDs and DVDs.

"With the passion of St Paul, we continue to find ever new ways of proclaiming the WORD."

Pauline
BOOKS & MEDIA

Christian Radio and TV

The Faisalabad Centre of PBCS started in 1962 under the leadership of a missionary, John Wilder. John also had the vision of a recording studio to prepare Christian radio programmes. A recording studio was built with technical help from the Far East Broadcasting Association (FEBA) in 1982. The Pakistan Christian Recording Ministries (PCRM) produces radio programmes and recordings of hymns and songs in Urdu, Punjabi and Saraiki to enrich the worship of the church in Pakistan. *"We are airing every day our audio programmes on shortwave radio, local FM station and on social media."* Each year about 12,000 responses are received from listeners.

PCRM is just one of several professional studios across Pakistan, preparing radio programmes in several languages, mostly to be broadcast by FEBA.

Since 2000 Christian cable television has also been launched in many areas of Pakistan. Jesus Christ Television (JCTV) was the nation's first Christian TV channel, which began in Lahore in 2004. It was followed in 2006 by Isaac TV under the ministry of Pastor Anwar Fazal. Several other Christian TV stations are now available – and all of them also broadcast worldwide on the internet.

Chapter 25

Hospitals, Schools and Businesses

Pakistan's Christians have made a great contribution to the nation since 1947. One of the greatest has been in schools and hospitals. We cannot write about them all, but have chosen just a few of the best. Thank God also for the others: Edwardes College in Peshawar, the Christian hospitals in Peshawar, Bannu, Tank and Quetta, the Women's Christian Hospital in Multan, the Cathedral Schools of the Church of Pakistan and Jesus and Mary Convent Schools. And many more.

The United Christian Hospital in Lahore

After Independence in 1947, thousands of families arrived in Pakistan from India. Many who managed to reach Pakistan were badly injured in riots. They travelled along the Ferozepur Road or by train to Walton Railway Station. Some Christians, many from Forman Christian College, took pity on these refugees and opened a temporary hospital in two of the students' hostels in FCC.

By 1950 the college needed its hostels back. Some missionaries and local Christians met to build an entirely new hospital. They bought land in Gulberg and an American architect, Le Young, designed the building. An engineer was needed to supervise the construction.

Mr Dan Bavington was in England and looking to work in Pakistan where he had spent part of his childhood. He was invited to supervise the building. Dan arrived in Lahore in December 1960 to oversee the construction of the new United Christian Hospital. He was joined in 1963 by his fiancée Ruth. They held their wedding reception on the UCH building site. It took four years to build as money became available. Meanwhile, the old hospital continued to function in F.C. College until 1964.

Pakistan's first open-heart surgery was performed in UCH in 1964. The 250-bed hospital trained nurses, lab and X-Ray technicians and served thousands of Pakistanis, both Christian and Muslim. Sadly, due to funding and other difficulties, the hospital failed to keep its high standard. Staff left and the hospital fell into disrepair. In 2018 the Chief Justice, Mian Saqib Nisar, ordered the hospital to be restored. *"This hospital is an icon of Lahore,"* he said. *"We want it to operate once again."* In 2020 a team of volunteers, led by Pastor Sajid Masih, began work to restore UCH to its former splendour.

After completing the UCH building, Dan Bavington and Dennis Norris founded the Christian construction company, Zor Engineers, specialising in buildings and structures. Since it began, Zor have built hundreds of buildings, both for Christian organisations and for many other clients.

Bach Christian Hospital, Qalandarabad

The greatest reason for opening the Bach Christian Hospital was *"to share God's love through compassionate and competent health care... and to help build the church of our Lord Jesus Christ".* The hospital was built on its present site in Qalandarabad in 1956. It was named Bach  Hospital in memory of Mr Thomas Bach, who spent 18 years as a missionary with The Evangelical Alliance Mission in South America.

Two missionaries from TEAM came to Hazara in the early 1950s. They looked in vain for a clinic or medical facilities for the local community but there was nothing. It led them to open a clinic in Mansehra in 1951. They continued to look for land to establish a permanent hospital. With the help of the District Commissioner in Muzaffarabad they finally purchased a large plot at Qalandarabad, and with his encouragement they began to build. The hospital finally opened in 1956.

As well as all the hospital buildings, arrangements were made for housing for staff and their families. For several years they had no water supply. Then they began to dig and were amazed when water began to flow. Now there is a Christian community outside the hospital with its own church. The hospital has 60 beds and 200 staff members. Every year about 90,000 patients come for treatment – and they do about 2,000 operations.

Kunri Christian Hospital

Kunri is a town in the Umarkot District of Sindh province about 170 miles from Karachi. There was no hospital in the area until a missionary began a mobile clinic that moved from village to village. He called it the "Caravan Hospital" because it operated from a mobile van. This was the vision of Dr Jock and Gwendy Anderson. They realised their dream in 1960 to bring eye surgery and general medical services to many thousands in Sindh.

In 1960, Bishop Chandu Ray was moved by the medical needs of the people in the rural Thar Desert. He began with a mobile eye clinic, which carried out free eye camps in different villages.

In 1962, with land purchased and buildings constructed, the Kunri Christian Hospital opened. Today, the hospital is jointly supported by the Church of Pakistan and the Roman Catholic Church. It once had 110 beds but this has since decreased.

Kinnaird College for Women

Kinnaird College was founded in 1913 by the Zenana and Bible Medical Mission, in co-operation with other missions. Its aim was to give Punjabi Christian women the opportunity to gain qualifications as teachers. It is named after Lady Mary Jane Kinnaird, the wife of a Scottish banker, and co-founder of the YWCA.

The college moved to its present site in 1933 and new buildings were constructed. Dr Mira Phailbus served as Principal for 32 years (see Chapter 23). In 2002, under her leadership, the college was given the status of a university and granted the licence to award degrees. It has a national reputation for educational excellence, and a widespread influence across all communities. Today more than 3,300 students are enrolled in the college.

Isabella McNair was Principal from 1928 to 1950. Under her leadership, Kinnaird College became one of the finest colleges in British India. This photo of the science lab was taken during her tenure as Principal.

St Anthony's High School, Lahore

St Anthony's was founded on 1st March 1892 in Empress Road, Lahore, by the Capuchin friars from Belgium. They named it St Anthony's Catholic Day School. There were just three students.

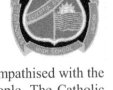

As it grew, it moved to Lawrence Road, and was renamed St Anthony's High School in 1900. The school was dedicated to St Anthony of Padua who sympathised with the poor and miserable and gave hope to despairing people. The Catholic Bishop of Lahore, Rt Reverend Van Don Bouch, performed the dedication ceremony.

Many notable Pakistanis studied at St Anthony's. The list of alumni is long, and includes two Prime Ministers (Nawaz Sharif and Shehbaz Sharif) and the former Governor of Punjab, Salmaan Taseer, who was murdered in 2011 for his outspoken criticism of the Blasphemy Laws and his defence of Christian Aasia Bibi. The nuclear physicist, Abdul Qadeer Khan (known as the "father of Pakistan's atomic weapons programme") studied at St Anthony's, as also did cricketers Rameez Raja and Majid Khan (both former captains of Pakistan's cricket team) – and many more distinguished leaders of Pakistani society.

Group Captain Cecil Chaudhry was also a graduate as well as Principal (see Chapter 23). Lawrence Road that runs past the school was renamed Cecil Chaudhry Road in his honour in 2014.

1972: Christian schools nationalised

On 15th March 1972 Prime Minister Zulfiqar Ali Bhutto nationalised many industries, schools and colleges (see Chapter 8), 118 of which were church-run institutions. Happily, many of them have since been returned to Christian ownership.

Chapter 26

Pastors, Theologians and Evangelists

Pakistani Christians in leadership

After Independence in 1947 the Pakistan Government continued to
recognise the valuable work being done by missionaries from other
countries. For many years missionaries have been given permission to
continue their work. The situation changed towards the end of the
twentieth century. However, since Independence, most churches and
Christian institutions have been led by Pakistanis. In this chapter we look
at just a few of the outstanding Christian leaders of churches, as well as
teachers of theology and the Bible.

Bishop Chandu Ray, who loved God and loved His Word

Chandu Ray was born in 1912 to a Hindu Sindhi family in Karachi. His
parents taught him the stories of the Hindu gods and took him to visit
their holy places. He studied Buddhism and Islam but they brought him
no peace. Then God met him and opened his eyes.

*"God called me out of the darkness of Hinduism
into his marvellous light...I had been with my
mother on pilgrimages all over India... Then I
met a Christian friend with eye disease who
asked me to read the Bible to him. I read John
chapter 14: 'I am the way, the truth and the life
... Ask what you will in my name and I will do it'.
We prayed in faith and God gave physical sight
to my friend and spiritual light to me."*

Chandu was a lover of books – he loved to read, and now he loved to give
books to others, especially the Bible. He studied theology, and prepared
himself to become a pastor. He was married in 1942 to Sarah, an orphan
girl from the Brenton Carey Orphanage in Karachi. The next year he was
ordained as a deacon in Christ Church, Karachi. In 1946 they moved to
Hyderabad, where he worked to win the Kohli people to Christ. Hundreds
became Christian.

Because of his great love of the Bible he joined the Bible Society as General Secretary in 1947. As he knew Sindhi, he published the Sindhi Old Testament and revised the New Testament. He also worked on the Bible in Tibetan. His translator, Yoseb, said: *"I have found Christ through the reading of Scriptures and so I want to give the people of Tibet the Bible in their mother tongue."*

In 1963 he became the first Bishop of Karachi, where he served for the next five years. In 1975 he joined the staff of the Haggai Institute in Singapore and later became their Director of Third World Outreach until his retirement in 1982. He died in 1983.

Ernest Mall, who lived a life of love and worship

Following the inspiration of Pastor I.D. Shahbaz (see Chapter 14), the Church in Pakistan has produced many wonderful worship songs and many great worship leaders. Among the best known and loved were Ernest Mall and Hizikiel Sarosh.

Pastor Ernest Mall was born in 1950 in Lahore. When he was only five years old his father taught him to sing. Later he led the choir in Naulakha Church in Lahore.

Ernest accepted the Lord Jesus Christ as his Lord and Saviour in 1967. He said that he met Jesus face to face in a dream when he was eight years old. *"I don't know a day in my life when I have not known the reality of the Lord Jesus Christ."*

"Along with his songs of praise and worship, his gentle spirit and kindness will always be remembered."

He went to live in America in 1975 to work as a teacher and businessman. He married Edwina in 1977. Then in 1987 God told him to use his voice to sing the praises of Jesus Christ. In the following years he composed and sang more than 500 Christian songs. He served as choir director for the Pakistani New Life Church in Philadelphia, USA – and then pastor of the Morning Star Christian Church. People remember him best when he came to Pakistan to take meetings and to sing. He died in 2008.

Dr Hizkiel Sarosh, pastor, poet and musician

Hizkiel Sarosh was born on 3rd April 1947 in Lahore. He gave his life to Christ at the age of 19 and was baptised in the River Ravi in 1965. The following year he married his cousin Maya Gill, with whom he had seven children.

After studying at the FGA Bible School, Dr Sarosh served as a Bible teacher at the same school from 1975 to 1998.

He was chairman of the Full Gospel Assemblies of Pakistan for many years and founding pastor of Pakistan's largest local church. He was a powerful preacher, pastor, poet, church planter, church administrator and musician, a role model to many aspiring pastors.

Dr Sarosh graduated in music from Punjab University with B.A (Hon). He was both a musician and a poet and wrote three poetry books and 675 Gospel worship songs, many of them well known and sung all over the world, especially in Pakistani churches.

Tribute to Hizkiel Sarosh in the *EXPRESS TRIBUNE*

"Members of his church and many pastors lined up to pay tribute to Sarosh. Several gospel singers presented their tribute in song and the church choir led in worship. They celebrated a life well lived and a race well run. Pastor Hizkiel Sarosh lived by what he wrote. And what he wrote moved hearts."

Hizkiel Sarosh was sadly killed in a car accident on 8th November 2015 in Pindi Bhattian on his way back from preaching at a meeting in Faisalabad. Many were present at his funeral, including members of the military, political figures, electronic and print media. He was buried in the Christian Cemetery, Lahore.

He was greatly missed by many.

Joseph Marie Anthony Cordeiro, Pakistan's first Roman Catholic Cardinal

Joseph Marie Anthony Cordeiro was the first Pakistani Cardinal of the Roman Catholic Church. He was born in 1918 in Bombay (India), educated at St Patrick's High School, Karachi, then at Bombay and Oxford universities. He received his religious training at the Papal Seminary in Kandy, Sri Lanka, and was ordained a priest in Karachi, Pakistan, in August 1946.

In 1950 he was appointed Vice Principal of St Patrick's High School, Karachi. He then served in Quetta before returning to Karachi as Archbishop at St Patrick's Cathedral.

In 1973 Pope Paul VI elevated him to the position of Cardinal. This meant he attended Conclaves, which are the private meetings of the Roman Catholic Church in Rome, Italy – like a parliament of about 200 senior priests. He received many honours due to his years of faithful service. He died from cancer on 11th February 1994 at the Holy Family Hospital.

Rev. Dr Aslam Ziai, a gifted theologian and Bible teacher

Aslam Ziai was born in 1948 in Gujranwala. His father, Siraj Din, was an agricultural labourer. As a boy he used to work with his father in the fields, while studying at the Islamiya High School in Gujranwala.

After getting his BA degree Aslam joined the staff of PFES (Pakistan Fellowship of Evangelical Students: see Chapter 24) in Karachi. He married Sudesh in 1973. For a time he worked as the director of Shalom Christian Centre in Jhelum, then with OTS (see Chapter 27) and the Bible Society. He also served as pastor of Crowe Chapel in Gujranwala (named after Rev. Osborne Crowe, director of CTTC, see Chapter 20).

Aslam's greatest passion was to study theology. He went for studies in Singapore, Gujranwala and Pittsburgh (USA) where he became a Doctor of Theology. Aslam continued to study throughout his life. In 1991 he was appointed Vice-Principal of Gujranwala Theological Seminary. Aslam was a great scholar and Bible teacher. He was the main speaker at the Sialkot Convention many times. He also wrote 15 books on the Old Testament prophets. He often said: *"I wish my students to be eager readers of the Bible and passionate servants of the Lord."* Sadly, Aslam died in 2013.

Dr K. L. Nasir, a great theologian and Bible teacher

Kundan Lall Nasir was born in 1918 in Jandialla Sheer Khan District, Sheikhupura. He studied at the Government High School in Chakwal, Murray College in Sialkot and Gordon College in Rawalpindi – and then at the United Presbyterian Theological Seminary in Gujranwala (now Gujranwala Theological Seminary). He also served as pastor in various villages in Punjab and in Kohat.

He was a great scholar of the Bible. In 1947 he joined the staff, and then became Principal, of Gujranwala Theological Seminary. He was a powerful preacher, and for 50 years spoke at Christian conventions all over the country. He also wrote many valuable theological books, a magazine, *Kalam-e-Haq*, a Bible atlas, Bible history and introductions to the Old Testament.

Due to his strong Christian convictions, he resigned from the seminary and in 1968 opened the Faith Theological Seminary in Gujranwala. This caused a tragic division in many Presbyterian churches. He died in 1996, but his legacy remains as one of Pakistan's greatest biblical theologians and teachers.

Frank Khair Ullah

Frank Khair Ullah was another great teacher, pastor and writer. He was born in 1914 in Nowshera. His father was an Afghan Christian who worked with the Church Missionary Society, and his mother was the daughter of an Afghan mullah, who worked on the translation of Psalms into Pushto. Frank took his Master's degree from F.C. College in 1933 and earned a PhD degree from the University of Edinburgh.

During World War II he served in the Indian Army as the secretary of the YMCA in the Middle East before joining Murray College in Sialkot as a lecturer of English language. He was the most popular teacher of poetry and drama. He had a wonderful sense of humour. In 1964 he became Principal for the next eight years.

He was ordained in the Church of Pakistan and served for several years as pastor of St Andrew's Church in Lahore. He also worked as the director of the creative writing project at Masihi Isha'at Khana (MIK), the Christian Publishing House. His final legacy was the production of *Qamoos al Kitab*, an Urdu Bible dictionary with more than 5,000 articles.

In 1994, he and his wife moved to Toronto, Canada, to live with their daughter. He continued his work there as a writer and died in 1997.

Chapter 27

Colleges and Seminaries, Equipping the Church

As the number of Christians increased in Sialkot in the nineteenth century, the Presbyterian mission realised they needed to train leaders for the church. In 1877 James Barr started a class to teach new converts the Bible and theology. This is how it began: *"A few students brought together and housed in small, one-room mud huts, the classes seated on verandas or under the shade of trees."* It was the beginning of the movement to train and equip godly Christians for leadership in the church.

Gujranwala Theological Seminary

The seminary that opened in Sialkot in 1877 with James Barr, Andrew Gordon and Rev. G.L. Thakur Das was very simple. The training only ran during the five summer months. The first four students graduated in 1882 and were ordained in 1886.

The classes moved from place to place for the convenience of the lecturers. Firstly it moved to Pasrur, then Jhelum, and later back to Sialkot. In 1912 the seminary moved to its present location in Gujranwala. Wazir Chand, a graduate of Gordon College, joined the seminary as a professor in 1928. He was an experienced teacher and pastor and became the first national principal of the seminary. He died in 1952.

After Pakistan gained its independence, the seminary opened its doors to students of many other churches. Methodists, Anglicans, Lahore Church Council and others sent students and provided staff as well as taking part in the managing Board. The second Pakistani principal was Dr K.L. Nasir (see Chapter 26) who held this position from 1958 until 1968.

Women's training: United Bible Training Centre (UBTC)

Across the road from the seminary is UBTC, a centre for training women in pastoral, biblical and evangelistic ministry. It was founded in response to a spiritual revival that took place in 1936 in the Mission Girls' High School in Pathankot. The Bible Training School opened in 1939 in Rawalpindi and moved onto land at the Gujranwala Theological Seminary in 1947. It offers short courses for nurses, teachers, pastors' wives and college students. Vivienne Stacey was a teacher and then Principal from 1955 for 20 years. Esther John studied there from 1957 to 1959 (see Chapter 19).

For those who cannot go to Bible School or Seminary: The Open Theological Seminary

Theological Education by Extension (TEE) is used all over the world for ordinary Christians to study the Bible, using course books, home study and in weekly groups. It began in Pakistan in 1971 with the initiative of a professor from Gujranwala Seminary as its coordinator. It later became known as PACTEE and then in 1989 the Open Theological Seminary (OTS).

OTS aims to equip its students for a lifetime of learning, to bring renewal to the church in Pakistan. Students should study to know the Bible and so be able to use their gifts in their churches and with the wider society.

Students can study at Discipleship level, Certificate level, Diploma level and Degree level. There are also courses for teenagers.

Training leaders for the Roman Catholic Church:

Christ the King Seminary, Karachi

Christ the King Seminary in Karachi has been described as *"the pioneering theological institution for the Catholic Church in Pakistan"*. It was the first and most important training college for the Catholic Church in Pakistan. It started in 1956 with only four students. Among their early students were several who went on to become leaders in the Church: Archbishop Lawrence Saldanha, Archbishop Evarist Pinto, Bishop Anthony Lobo, Joseph Cardinal Coutts, and Bishop John Joseph of Faisalabad.

Hundreds of priests from Pakistan and many other countries have been trained at the seminary. Since 1997 the seminary has offered courses leading to a diploma in theology, as well as programmes for lay people involved in church ministries.

St Francis Xavier Seminary, Youhannabad, Lahore

St Francis Xavier Seminary is a Roman Catholic seminary in Youhannabad, Lahore. It opened in September 1994, and offers a two-year programme in Christian, Greek and Islamic Philosophy. It is affiliated to the Pontifical Urban University of Rome.

The St Francis Xavier School inside the seminary serves the children of the poor, where the seminarians also teach the catechism and English. The building is surrounded by a fairly large piece of land, which includes a football ground, a basketball court and a Marian shrine.

Zarephath Bible Seminary (ZBS), Rawalpindi

In 1976 seven church leaders met together to pray and discuss the need for more trained Pakistani Christian workers. From this discussion came the Zarephath Bible Seminary in 1982. The name Zarephath was taken from 1 Kings 17:9, which states the vision of the founders to prepare fully capable ministers for God's service.

These seven Christian missions and churches began classes in the city of Attock in the north-west corner of Punjab. In 1998 the school moved from Attock City to the present location in Rawalpindi to provide evening classes for Christians in the area. About 80 students study in all programmes. Since the beginning of ZBS, 95% of its graduates are in Christian ministry. The college is led by a Pakistani principal, supported by a national staff with qualified guest lecturers.

The ZBS purpose statement is:

"To train students to become Christ-like servant leaders through coming to know the indwelling, risen Lord Jesus Christ more deeply and personally."

The Full Gospel Assembly (FGA) Bible Seminary, Lahore

The FGA Bible School was founded in 1967 by a Swedish missionary, Rev. Kjell Sjøberg. The Pentecostal movement was growing rapidly, and there was an urgent need for more full-time pastors and evangelists to be trained.

The Bible School started with a one-year course to prepare men and women for full-time ministry. Dr Liaquat Qaiser became Principal of the Bible School in 1987, and then introduced the two-year Bachelor of Theology degree programme.

More than 700 students have graduated from the school and are now serving as pastors, evangelists, indigenous missionaries, children's ministry workers, women's ministry workers, worship leaders, and also as witnesses in secular professions. Graduates serve with FGA churches, other Pentecostal and Evangelical churches, and parachurch organisations. Some are key leaders in their churches or organisations, an instrument of blessing to tens of thousands in Pakistan today.

It is now known as the FGA Bible Seminary.

There are many other Bible and theological colleges in Pakistan. We cannot tell all their stories. The Roman Catholic Church has six seminaries to train priests. There are several large Protestant and Evangelical colleges, such as the Church of Pakistan's St Thomas' Theological College in Karachi and the Lahore College of Theology in Lahore. There are also many smaller colleges: the Assemblies of God Bible College, Lahore, and the Bible Training Centre run by the Brethren churches, and many more.

Chapter 28

Christians in Crisis and Suffering

Increasing problems for Christians

In many ways Pakistan's Christians have lived in freedom and with great blessing since Pakistan became independent in 1947. The dream of Quaid-e-Azam, Mohammad Ali Jinnah, was that Pakistan should be a country that respected every religion equally. *"You are free to go to your temples; free to go to your mosques or to any other places of worship in the State of Pakistan,"* he said.

However, after his death in 1948, the Islamic parties insisted on a greater emphasis on Pakistan as an Islamic state. Finally, the 1956 Constitution of Pakistan was published, in which the country was named an Islamic Republic. It was the beginning of Pakistan's increasing Islamisation. However, the Constitution continued to give full freedom, respect and rights to Christians and all minorities. Article 18(a) and (b) of the Constitution declared:

"Every citizen has the right to profess, practise and propagate any religion; and every religious denomination and every sect thereof has the right to establish, maintain and manage its religious institutions."

However, as a result of changes in government, the war in Afghanistan and other things, Christians were often treated as second-class citizens. During the rule of General Muhammad Zia ul-Haq (1977–1988) Islamic parties gained greater power and control.

In 1982 and 1986, two new clauses were added to Section 295 of the Pakistan Penal Code. The Blasphemy Law made insulting the Qur'an or the Muslim Prophet punishable by imprisonment or death. This law has often been used falsely against Christians.

Facing discrimination

Many Pakistani Christians have experienced discrimination as a result of the growing confidence of Pakistan's pride in an Islamic identity. Many Christians fear the threat of the Blasphemy Law, which has undermined the relationship between Christians and Muslims. Some have faced clear discrimination in their school or college, in job applications and career promotions. Many have been insulted by being called "sweeper" or "*chuhra*". There have been false blasphemy accusations, religiously motivated murders, kidnappings, forced conversions, and instances of intimidation. Sadly, many Christians feel that there is no future for Christians in Pakistan.

Shanti Nagar – the House of Peace

Shanti Nagar is a village in southern Punjab, six miles from Khanewal. It was founded by the Salvation Army in 1916, and most of the 15,000 people living there are Christians. There is one mosque and several churches.

On the night of 5th February 1997, the 27th night of Ramazan, faithful Muslims in Khanewal had gathered for a night of prayer. Someone spread a rumour that torn pages of the Qur'an were found in Shanti Nagar. The report travelled very quickly through mosques and loudspeakers throughout the area.

The next day, 6th February at nine o'clock in the morning, a crowd of 30,000 Muslims attacked Shanti Nagar. They were armed with axes, daggers, sticks, pistols and shotguns. They destroyed everything. They appeared to be well organised. They entered houses and stole all valuable objects before setting fire to the rest. They burnt shops, houses and churches together with Bibles, religious books and furniture.

Thirteen churches and three schools were burned in Shanti Nagar; 775 houses were also burned out, and ten shops were destroyed in Khanewal. Amazingly, no one was killed. Christians from all over Pakistan visited Shanti Nagar with money, food and other items. Bishop John Joseph visited the village on 21ˢᵗ February and gave assurance for every possible help.

Khorian and Gojra

On the evening of 30ᵗʰ July 2009 a mob attacked the Christian community in Khorian, a village in Toba Tek Singh District. They were accused of desecrating pages of the Qur'an. The armed mob burned 57 homes, stole their belongings and destroyed the churches.

Another mob attacked a Christian colony in Gojra city on 1ˢᵗ August 2009. They set fire to 68 houses and killed seven Christians, including three women and two children. Christian witnesses said that the police were present but did nothing to protect the Christians. Pakistan's federal minister for minorities, Shahbaz Bhatti, visited Gojra and asked the police to provide protection for Christians who were facing threats.

The police ultimately arrested dozens of suspects, yet no one was ever brought to trial or imprisoned.

The tragedy and the sorrow

On 22nd September 2013 two suicide bombers attacked All Saints Church in Peshawar (see Chapter 13). The two men struck at the end of a Sunday service. The suicide bombing killed at least 85 people and 140 others were wounded. A school teacher, Nazir

Khan, said the service had just ended and at least 400 worshippers were greeting each other when there was a huge explosion. *"A huge blast threw me on the floor. I saw wounded people everywhere,"* Khan said. Pages of a Bible were scattered near the altar.

Sadly, this was not all. On 15th March 2015, suicide bombers attacked St John Catholic Church and Christ Church (Church of Pakistan) in

Youhannabad, Lahore, during the Sunday service. They tried to enter the churches but were stopped at the gate, where they blew themselves up.

One young man, Akash Bashir, stopped a suicide bomber who was trying to enter the Catholic Church. *"I will die but I will not let you go in,"* he reportedly told the terrorist. The attacker then set off his bomb, immediately killing himself and Akash. Fifteen people were killed and 70 were wounded in the attacks.

Other attacks on Christians have brought sorrow and fear to the Christian community. On 9th March 2013 an angry mob set ablaze more than 150 houses of Christians in Lahore's Joseph Colony to take revenge for a blasphemy allegedly committed by a Christian two days earlier.

Aasia Bibi and the Blasphemy Law

In June 2009, Aasia Bibi, a Christian, had an argument with her co-workers while working in the fields. A few days later they accused her of saying blasphemous words. She was arrested and imprisoned. In November 2010, a Sheikhupura judge sentenced her to death. The verdict was upheld by the Lahore High Court.

Her family went into hiding after receiving death threats. Finally, after 11 years in prison, on 31st October 2018, the Supreme Court of Pakistan acquitted Noreen. She and her family left the country and sought asylum in Canada.

Bishop John Joseph: a faithful martyr

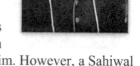

John Joseph was born in Khushpur in 1932. He received his religious education at Christ the King Seminary in Karachi and was ordained in Faisalabad in 1960. He became a teacher at the seminary. On 9th January 1984 he became Bishop of Faisalabad. A great human rights advocate and an outstanding biblical scholar, he was working with the Bible Society revision committee.

In 1998, a young Christian, Ayub Masih, was accused of blasphemy. Bishop John Joseph believed he was innocent and set out to defend him. However, a Sahiwal civil court found him guilty and sentenced him to death.

The Blasphemy Laws were often used wrongly against innocent people. John Joseph was so angry about Ayub Masih's death sentence that he went to Sahiwal to protest. On 6th May he shot himself outside the courthouse and so became a martyr. He was buried in Khushpur.

Shahbaz Bhatti: courage and principle

Also buried in Khushpur is another brave Christian. Shahbaz Bhatti was born in Lahore in 1968. He founded APMA (the All Pakistan Minorities Alliance) in 2002.

He was elected as a member of the National Assembly in 2008 and became Federal Minister for Minorities Affairs in 2008. When Aasia Bibi was sentenced to death he spoke out against the Blasphemy Laws and in support of Aasia. For this he was murdered in his car near his mother's home on 2nd March 2011. *"I believe in Jesus Christ who has given His own life for us ... and I will die to defend their rights,"* he said.

Terrorism in Pakistan

Christians are not the only ones who have suffered from terrorism in Pakistan in recent years. The terrorist attack on the Army Public School in Peshawar in 2014 resulted in the death of 149 people, including 132 school children, all of them Muslims.

The tragedy in Jaranwala

Jaranwala is a town of medium size in Faisalabad District in central Punjab, with a population of about 200,000. It is famous for the production of rice, wheat, sugarcane, vegetables and fruit.

Early in the morning of 16ᵗʰ August 2023 a mosque loudspeaker in Jaranwala announced that torn pages of the Qur'an had been found with blasphemous content on them near a church. A mob gathered and began to attack churches and Christian homes. A police official said: *"The crowd consisted mostly of young men, teenagers, wielding batons, sticks. By 9 or 10am, as passions were running high, they attacked the churches and homes of Christians."*

"Words fail me as I write this... A church building is being burnt as I type this message. Bibles have been desecrated and Christians have been falsely accused of violating the Holy Quran. We cry out for justice..."

Bishop Azad Marshall

It was reported that about 1,200 violent young men set out to destroy 22 churches, damaging them or setting them on fire. A hundred Christian homes were also either completely or partially damaged. One report said that *"the incident was unprecedented in magnitude and ferocity"*.

Muslim leaders condemned the attack and the Government promised to compensate the losses and rebuild the churches. 100 arrests were made. But the confidence of the Christian community was shattered once again.

In times of earthquake and floods

Though Christians have often suffered at the hands of religious extremists, it must also be remembered how the Christian community has responded in times of national disaster.

On 8th October 2005 an earthquake struck Azad Kashmir. More than 86,000 people died, and millions lost their homes. Christians were among the first to offer aid and to serve the thousands who suffered.

In response to the many children and young people traumatised by the disaster through the deaths of family members or friends, Christian aid agencies provided counselling and care centres specifically for children. Pakistan Caritas, World Vision International and many other Christian agencies were quick to provide relief and reconstruction. *"The emergency has allowed cultural barriers to come down and this is the time to build trust."*

Kunhar Christian Hospital is a mission hospital, staffed exclusively by Pakistani Christians, serving a poor local population and exemplifying Christian compassion and self-sacrifice. Located in Ghari Habibullah, close to the epicentre of the earthquake, it brought relief to many.

Pakistan's Christians have also been quick to help during the great floods of 2010 and 2022. The Catholic Mission Society of St Columban reported that *"mosquitos are everywhere, causing more and more people to get sick with malaria"*. The Society was able to provide food, temporary shelter and access to clean water.

A Pastor pleaded for help: *"People lost their livestock, houses, crops and many things. Many are in huts and tents without enough warm clothes and blankets. I have been praying and looking for blankets, warm clothes and tents. God is good all the time."* Help was provided.

Chapter 29

God's Amazing Love for Pakistan

Pope John Paul II visited Karachi

16th February 1981 is a day that few of Karachi's Christians will forget. Pope John Paul II visited Karachi. As he came down from his aircraft at Karachi airport, the Pope knelt down and kissed Pakistani soil. His kiss was a testimony to this land being sacred.

He was met at the airport by the President, General Mohammad Zia ul-Haq (see picture), and travelled to the National Stadium to celebrate Mass for approximately 100,000 Christians who had gathered to greet him. St Patrick's High School band welcomed the Pope to the stadium. In his speech the Pope appealed for closer ties between Christianity and Islam. He said: *"I pray that mutual understanding and respect between Christians and Muslims will continue and grow deeper."* The Mass was shown on national television.

About 15 minutes before the Pope arrived at the stadium, a powerful bomb exploded behind the VIP stand at the stadium, killing the man carrying the bomb. The Pope was not told about the bomb, and his short three-hour visit was celebrated peacefully by Karachi's Christians.

Pakistan and the worldwide Marches for Jesus

In May 1987 a group of Christians in England organised a prayer and praise march through the streets of London. They walked through the city, singing  and praying. This march became an international event. In 1994 10 million people marched in the streets of more than a thousand cities in 178 nations around the world to the glory and praise of God.

In Pakistan too, many marches were organised. Hundreds of Christians came together in different cities. They walked through the streets, often alongside a decorated truck, stopping to preach, sing and pray for the city and the government.

The highlight of Pakistan's Marches for Jesus took place in 1999. Christians hired a railway train, filled it with enthusiastic believers, and travelled from Peshawar in the north to Karachi. The train stopped at stations along the route, with prayers and preaching to the crowds at the station, and organised marches through the city streets.

Christ the King

Roman Catholic churches in many of Pakistan's cities celebrate the Feast of Christ the King with a procession or parade. It started in Karachi in 1926 and was held every year for 41 years. It was held for 110 years in Khushpur.

A procession with dramas that illustrated scenes from Bible stories highlighted the celebration in Khushpur. *"Last year we performed 20 stories, this year we had more,"* said a shopkeeper. *"Many residents join the celebrations."*

"We have waited for this day the whole year. Villagers from all over the country returned home to join the Christ the King procession," said Mazhar Bhatti, one of the 1,000 Christians taking part.

Palm Sunday and Easter processions

Many churches across Pakistan celebrate Palm Sunday with processions through the streets, waving palm branches and singing songs of praise. More processions begin by candle-light early on Easter morning to welcome the Resurrection of Christ from the dead.

A giant cross stands tall in the centre of Karachi

The huge 140-foot cross was the vision of a Pakistani Christian businessman, Parvez Henry Gill. Constructed in 2014, it stands in the Christian Cemetery.

Pervez claimed to have heard God asking him to do something for the Christian community four years before. He decided to build Asia's largest cross. He said:

"The cross will be a symbol of God, and everybody who sees this will be worry-free. It is to prompt Christians to stay in Pakistan and do something for their community."

Sialkot Convention – celebrating 100 years

All over Pakistan many churches now hold annual conventions – meetings of Christians, with worship and Gospel preaching. They all began with the great convention at Sialkot in 1904 (see Chapter 17). The photos are from the conventions in 1912 and 2016.

Thousands attend great Christian meetings

In recent years many open-air evangelistic meetings have been held in different parts of Pakistan. Many have been led by anointed evangelists from overseas. One of these, Dr Marilyn Hickey, has visited Pakistan many times. She claimed to have preached to over 1 million people in Karachi. She reported: *"Hundreds of people were saved. A man was saved called Anwar Fazal."*

Pastor Anwar Fazal came to Christ in one of her meetings in 1995. He launched his Eternal Life Ministry in 2001 and Isaac TV in 2006 (see Chapter 24). Every Sunday 15,000 people worship in his church in Lahore.

All this tells us: the church is alive and well in Pakistan, and Pakistan's Christians have a great future

Chapter 30

The Future for Pakistan's Christians

2,000 years of Christian history – and beyond

In this book we have looked back over 2,000 years of Christian history in the land that we now call Pakistan. You have read that there have been Christians in Punjab and Sindh since the Apostle Thomas arrived in the Kingdom of Gondophares in the first century. Sometimes there were very few and life was very difficult. The story has been full of failure and success. But when we look at the church today, we must be amazed. Churches everywhere! Meetings attended by thousands! Hospitals and schools that carry the name of Christ! Christians in leadership across the land!

Beautiful church buildings

The largest official church in Pakistan is the Roman Catholic Church. It is made up of seven church units – two archdioceses, four dioceses, and one apostolic vicariate. They make up about half the total Christian population in Pakistan.

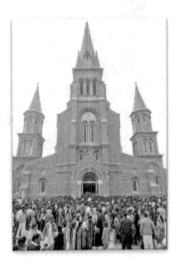

The second largest church is the Church of Pakistan, divided into eight areas known as dioceses. The Presbyterian Church of Pakistan is governed by a committee known as the synod. Then there are many smaller, but often more active churches, the Pentecostal churches, Salvation Army, the Brethren, the Baptists and many more.

Most of these different churches work well together and believe the same essential truths of the Gospel of Jesus Christ. They all come together for large events like the conventions (see Chapter 29).

There are beautiful church buildings in many parts of Pakistan today. The Catholic Sacred Heart Cathedral in Lahore is filled with worshippers. St Peter's Church in Karachi, opened in 2012, holds 5,000. St Matthew's Church in Nathia Gali is one of the most beautiful.

But it is people – Christians with faith in Christ – who are the future of the church in Pakistan

The future of Christianity in Pakistan

For too long, Christians in Pakistan have come to be known as a "sweeper" community. A lady called Shakeela reported in the *Daily Times* newspaper (2020): *"These people call us Bhanghi, Chuhra, Safai Wala (cleaner). I felt hurt. I cried and asked myself, how can they use these offensive words?"* Christians have been given the dirtiest jobs. Among Pakistan's sanitation workers, 80% are Christians. This has to stop. There is dignity and respect in being Christian.

There are many wealthy, successful and educated Christians in Pakistan, but the majority remain low-income labourers, domestic servants, landless farm and brick-kiln workers. Sadly, many Christians are exploited and abused. Organisations like the Human Rights Commission of Pakistan and the Jinnah Institute have done much to highlight injustices against Christians. Several Christian human rights lawyers, politicians and journalists have also done much to improve the status of Christians in Pakistan.

Christians and the independent churches

There are many large churches across Pakistan, especially in the cities. However, there are even more churches in majority Christian *bastis* (slums), homes, villages and brick kilns that do not belong to any of the large church denominations. A pastor who visits some of these village churches wrote: *"These Christians do not*

attend the church – there is no church in their area. We regularly share the Word of God among those people." Across Pakistan there are thousands of such small groups of Christian believers who meet together in a home or in the open air for worship. They receive basic teaching – often with a Pentecostal emphasis on the power of God – and love to sing.

Christian organisations and missions

In recent years hundreds of Christians, with vision and a desire to help their community, have started organisations. Some have received help from overseas, others have struggled to find funding for their own mission. As missionaries have left the country, many amazing people have taken their place, arranging seminars, conferences and campaigns.

The Pak Mission Society, founded by Adeel Rehmat in 2008 and based in Islamabad, has done extensive aid and relief work. The Human Friends Organisation, founded by

Sajid Christopher in Lahore in 2003, promotes religious freedom and inter-religious harmony. Many other such Christian organisations are active in working for the benefit of Pakistani society.

For a Better World

An informal survey of low-cost private schools in Punjab and Karachi was carried out in 2016. It collected details from 604 schools, run by Christians to serve poorer Christian communities.

It found evidence that there are probably up to 2,000 such small schools, poorly equipped, with untrained teachers on low salaries, trying to educate Christian children.

Schools:
Educating, equipping and preparing Christians for the future

We have written about the huge contribution of missionaries and Christians to provide education through high-quality schools and colleges (see Chapters 8, 15 and 25). Christians have built some of Pakistan's finest schools: F.C. College, The Church of Pakistan Cathedral Schools, the Convent of Jesus and Mary Schools, the Catholic and Presbyterian Board of Education schools – and many more run by the Full Gospel Assemblies, the Brethren and others.

But thousands of other Christians, unable to pay the fees or get access to these mission schools, have opened their own informal schools in villages, *bastis* and homes. Across Pakistan, pastors and parents – Christians with a passion and a vision to serve their community – have opened

small primary and high schools. Through these schools thousands of Christians are being prepared for their future in Pakistani society.

Looking back over 2,000 years

We can now look back to the arrival of the three kings at Bethlehem to worship the new-born baby in the manger. We do not know if one of those kings, Caspar, was from Punjab, but it is possible. Nor can we be sure that there were Punjabis in Jerusalem on the Day of Pentecost.

We do not know for sure whether the ancestors of Pakistan's Christians helped to build the cities of Mohenjodaro and Harappa. We cannot be sure about the ministry of the Apostle Thomas in Sirkap near Taxila, but it is probable.

But this we do know: there have been Christian believers in this land for many hundreds of years. And there will be increasing numbers of Christian believers in the years to come. Christians bring light and hope to the nation, and as loyal citizens will work for the prosperity and future of Pakistan.

Bibliography

This book has been largely a collection of many amazing documents and books that are publicly available. Most of the information is available online and you can do extensive research on Google. The stories I have collected can all be expanded, and the story becomes even more amazing.

I owe special credit to the Open Theological Seminary (Lahore) Church History Course written by Freda Carey and Majeed Abel, and available to OTS students in Urdu. Much of their research has also been taken from other sources. We all stand on the shoulders of giants.

This Bibliography contains some of the sites that have helped me, but is not exclusive – search and you will find many more.

Chapter 1   **Introduction: The Amazing Story**

The sons of Noah:
www.biblemapper.com/blog/index.php/2022/08/15/table-of-nations-shems-descendants/

Chapter 2   **Punjabis in the New Testament**

John of Hildersheim:
www.blackcentraleurope.com/sources/1000-1500/the-legend-of-the-three-kings-1483/

www.reliquarian.com/tag/john-of-hildesheim/

Chapter 3   **The Apostle Thomas in Taxila**

John Rooney: *Shadows in the Dark* (Christian Study Centre, Islamabad 1984)

William Barclay: *The Master's Men* (SCM Press Ltd. 1959)

The Acts of Thomas: http://www.gnosis.org/library/actthom.htm

Dr Michael Nazir-Ali:
https://michaelnazirali.com/articles/app/archive/02-2023/

Chapter 4   **Christians in Punjab for 1,000 Years**

Bar Sauma: www.depts.washington.edu/silkroad/texts/sauma.html

The Cross of Kovardo:
www.uobs.edu.pk/index.php/16-news/76-kowardo-cross

Chapter 5   **Christians and the Mughal Emperors**

John Rooney: *The Hesitant Dawn* (Christian Study Centre, Islamabad 1984)

Chapter 6   **The Arrival of Foreigners**

Abdul Masih:
https://www.fulcrum-anglican.org.uk/articles/abdul-masih-icon-of-indian-indigeneity/

www.academia.edu/37296099/Missionaries_Christianity_and_Education_in_19_th_Century_Punjab

Chapter 7   **The Great Bible Translators**

George Smith: *The Life of William Carey, Shoemaker & Missionary* (E-Artnow 2020)

Henry Martyn:
John Sargent: *Life and Letters of Henry Martyn* (Banner of Truth 1986)

www.evangelical-times.org/henry-martyn-pioneer-missionary/

http://ctrendsmag.com/sections/spotlight/celebrate-the-word-200-years-of-the-punjabi-bible/

Collected works of John C. Lowrie
John Lowrie: *Travels in North India* (Presbyterian Board of Publication 1842) www.logcollegepress.com/john-cameron-lowrie

Chapter 8   **The Missionaries Who Opened Schools**

J.C. Lowrie: *A Historical Sketch of the Board of Foreign Missions of the Presbyterian Church: 1837–1888*

John C. Lowrie: *Travels in North India* (Presbyterian Board of Publication 1842)

www.apnaorg.com/prose-content/english-articles/page-178/article-9/index.html

Dr Henry Forman: *A Sketch of the Life of Dr Forman*
www.friendsofforman.org/SiteFiles/CMS/Files/History-of-FCC-Dr.-Charles-Forman.pdf

Chapter 9   The 1857 War of Independence

Michael Edwardes: *Red Year: The Indian Rebellion of 1857* (Cardinal 1975)

www.rediff.com/news/special/the-forgotten-brutality-of-the-1857-mutiny/20170814.htm

https://www.thebetterindia.com/255573/skull-alum-bheg-1857-sepoy-soldier-british-colonial-india-english-pub-independence-struggle-sialkot-pakistan-history-div200/

www.victorianweb.org/history/empire/india/72.html

Chapter 10   Andrew Gordon and the Sialkot Mission

Andrew Gordon: *Our India Mission* (Andrew Gordon 1886)

William B. Anderson & Charles R. Watson: *Far North in India* (The Board of Foreign Missions of the United Presbyterian Church of North America: Philadelphia 1909)

Chapter 11   Spiritual Awakening Among the Meghs

Andrew Gordon: *Our India Mission* (Andrew Gordon 1886)

www.defence.pk/pdf/threads/mass-conversion-to-christianity-a-case-study-of-chuhra-community-in-sialkot-district-1880-1930.621980/

Annual Report of the Board of Foreign Missions of the United Presbyterian Church of North America (1906)

Chapter 12   Ditt and the Chuhra Revival

https://www.thefreelibrary.com/Mass+Conversion+To+Christianity%3A+A+Case+Study+Of+Chuhra+Community+In...-a0547875167

http://herald.dawn.com/news/1153539

Chapter 13   1850–1900 : Churches and Missions

Vivienne Stacey: *Thomas Valpy French* (Christian Study Centre 1982)

Eugene Stock: *An Heroic Bishop, the Story of French of Lahore* (Hodder & Stoughton 1914)

Chapter 14   1850–1900 : Some Outstanding Missionaries, Pastors and Evangelists

I.D. Shahbaz
www.thefreelibrary.com/A+precious+gift%3a+the+Punjabi+Psalms+and+the+legacy+of+Imam-ud-Din...-a0355557309

The Life of The Rev. Mawlawi Dr Imad ud-Din Lahiz:
www.answering-islam.org/Testimonies/mawlawi.html and
www.archive.org/details/ldpd_10987304_000/page/n19/mode/2up

Centenary Volume of the Church Missionary Society 1799–1899 (CMS 1902)

Eugene Stock: *The History of the Church Missionary Society, Volume 4* (CMS London 1916)

Rev. John F.W. Youngson: *Forty Years of the Punjab Mission of the Church of Scotland 1855–1895* (R & R Clark Ltd., Edinburgh 1896)

Missionaries and pastors together:
http://nearly-midnight.blogspot.com/2011/09/punjab-and-sind-at-1900-approx-from.html

Chapter 15   1850–1900 : Christian Schools and Hospitals

T.L. Pennell: *Among the Wild Tribes of the Afghan Frontier* (Seeley Service & Co. Limited 1909)
https://www.gutenberg.org/files/32231/32231-h/32231-h.htm

Henry Martyn Clark: *Robert Clark of the Punjab* (Andrew Melrose 1907)

Kasmir's Christian Heroines: https://kashmirlife.net/kashmirs-christian-heroines-issue-15-vol-12-240182/

Eugene Stock: *The History of the Church Missionary Society, Vol. 1–4* (Church Mission Society 1899, 1913)

Chapter 16   Christian Communities and the Canal Colonies

Robert Clark: *The Missions of the CMS in the Punjab and Sindh* (Church Missionary Society 1904)

Henry Martyn Clark: *Robert Clark of the Panjab* (Andrew Melrose 1907)

R. Maconachie: *Roland Bateman* (Church Missionary Society 1917)

Samuel Martin: https://www.pakistanchristian.org/our-personal-connection

https://openresearch-repository.anu.edu.au/handle/1885/112646

https://medium.com/@indochristianculture/the-pakistani-christian-how-a-community-was-born-d8aa265b6ab4

Bakht Singh: http://www.brotherbakhtsingh.org/briefbio.html

Chapter 17   Spiritual Revival in Punjab

St George De Lautour Booth-Tucker: *Darkest India* (Project Gutenberg Ebook 2004)

Emma Dean Anderson & Mary Jane Campbell: *In the Shadow of the Himalayas* (United Presbyterian Board of Foreign Missions 1942)

Frederick & Margaret Stock: *People Movements in the Punjab* (William Carey Library 1975)

Ed. Captain E.G. Carré: *Praying Hyde* (Pickering & Inglis)

Chapter 18   1900–1947 : Growing Churches Everywhere

Annual Report of the Board of Foreign Missions of the United Presbyterian Church of North America: 1911

John Rooney: *On Heels of Battles* (Christian Study Centre, Rawalpindi 1986)

John Rooney: *Into Deserts* (Christian Study Centre, Rawalpindi 1986)

Frederick & Margaret Stock: *People Movements in the Punjab* (William Carey Library 1975)

Ella M. Weatherley: *From West to East* (Zenana Bible & Medical Mission 1910)

Elizabeth Bielby: https://unchsl.tumblr.com/post/153860979172/in-1885-elizabeth-bielbys-thesis-entitled-the

The Comity Agreement:
https://archive.org/details/reportofpunjabmi00punj

A. Russell: *Marvellously Helped: The Trials and Triumphs of Blanche Brenton Carey* (Amazon 2022)

Chapter 19   1900–1947 : Christian Leaders Who Made a Difference

Sadhu Sundar Singh:
http://www.ccminternational.org/English/who_said_that/sadhu%20sundar%20singh.htm

Barakat Ullah:
https://www.answering-islam.org/Testimonies/baraktullah.html

Esther John: https://www.westminster-abbey.org/abbey-commemorations/commemorations/esther-john

https://www.westminster-abbey.org/about-the-abbey/history/modern-martyrs

Sultan Mohammad Paul:
http://path-of-peace.org/WhyIBecameAChristian.htm

Chapter 20   Some Great Christian Organisations

CTTC: https://cttc.edu.pk/

https://www.rekhta.org/publishers/punjab-religious-book-society-lahore-1/ebooks?ref=web&filter=book-publishers

Pakistan Bible Society: https://pbs.org.pk/

Cyril Davey: *Caring Comes First: Story of the Leprosy Mission* (HarperCollins 1987)

Chapter 21   1947 : Christians and Pakistan's Independence

Pakistan Journal of Social Sciences (PJSS) (Vol. 32, No. 2 (2012), pp. 437-443) The Role of Christians in the Freedom Movement of Pakistan: An Appraisal

G.M. Naaman: *My Grace is Sufficient for You* (The Good Way Publishing 2010)

Samuel Martin Burke:
https://www.thenews.com.pk/tns/detail/568846-christians-partitioned-punjab

PAF'S gallant Christian heroes:
https://www.brecorder.com/news/40216322

Chapter 22   The Growth of Churches Across Pakistan

Pentecostal churches:
https://www.suvarthamagazine.org/kjsamuel.html

Full Gospel Assemblies – Kjell Sjoberg: https://silo.tips/download/the-life-of-kjell-sjberg

www.catholicsinpakistan.org/

Ken & Jeanette Newton, editors: *The Brethren Movement Worldwide – Key information 2019* (Opal Trust 2019)

Autobiography of Bro. Bakht Singh (Genesis Publishing, India 2008)

Chapter 23   Pakistani Christians in National Leadership

Cecil Choudhry: https://www.hilal.gov.pk/eng-article/detail/NjE1Nw==.html

Aasiya Nasir: https://www.pakistanchristianpost.com/head-line-news-details/2948

Vivienne Stacey: *More Alive than Ever: The Story of Tara Joy James* (Pakistan Bible Society 2004)

Mira Phailbus: https://www.jworldtimes.com/old-site/css-exclusive/exclusive-interview/exclusive-interview-with-dr-mira-phailbus/

Justice Alvin Cornelius: http://justicecornelius.com/About.html

Michael Nazir-Ali:
https://michaelnazirali.com/articles/app/archive/02-2023/

Chapter 24   The Great Christian Ministries

Pakistan Fellowship of Evangelical Students (PFES): https://pfes.tripod.com/

Pakistan campus Crusade for Christ: https://pakccc.org/

Scripture Union Pakistan: https://scriptureunion.pk/

Masihi Isha'at Khana (MIK): https://mik.org.pk/

Dennis Clark: http://www.brow.on.ca/Articles/ClarkRev.htm

PBCS: https://www.pbcipk.org/

Nirali Kitaben: https://www.facebook.com/niralikitabentrust/

Daughters of St. Paul: https://www.paoline.org/site/52-years-in-pakistan/?lang=en

Pakistan Christian Recording Ministries: http://pakistan.kcm.co.kr/pcrm/introduction.html

Jesus Christ Television Pakistan (JCTV): https://www.jctvpak.tv/

Isaac TV: https://isaactelevision.tv/

Chapter 25   Hospitals, Schools and Businesses

United Christian Hospital, Lahore (UCH): https://www.unitedchristianhospitallahore.org/

ZOR Engineers (Pvt) Ltd: http://zor.com.pk/

Bach Christian Hospital: https://team.org/initiatives/bach-christian-hospital

Kunri Christian Hospital: https://dailytimes.com.pk/393766/the-silent-ruin-and-decay-of-the-amreeki-aspatal/

Kinnaird College for Women: https://www.kinnaird.edu.pk/

St Anthony's High School, Lahore: https://en.wikipedia.org/wiki/St._Anthony_High_School,_Lahore

Chapter 26   Pastors, Theologians and Evangelists

Chandu Ray:
www.stfrancismagazine.info/ja/images/pdf/vivienne/ChanduRay.pdf

Ernest Mall: https://www.facebook.com/OfficialErnestMall/

Hizkiel Sarosh: https://tribune.com.pk/story/996061/in-memoriam-the-legacy-of-a-faithful-servant

Cardinal Joseph Cordeiro:
https://en.wikipedia.org/wiki/Joseph_Cordeiro

Rev. Aslam Ziai:
https://ihtshamravi.wordpress.com/2013/05/26/unforgettable-ziai/

Dr K.L. Nasir: https://www.injeeli.com/writers/nasir-dr-k-l-1918-1996

Frank Khairullah – Qamoos al Kitab:
https://archive.org/details/qamoosalkitaburdudictionaryofbible/page/n25/mode/2up

Chapter 27   Colleges and Seminaries, Equipping the Church

Gujranwala Theological Seminary: http://www.gtspk.org/

United Bible Training Centre (UBTC):
https://www.facebook.com/profile.php?id=100082037111487
https://en.wikipedia.org/wiki/Vivienne_Stacey

The Open Theological Seminary (OTS): https://ots-trust.org/

Christ the King Seminary:
https://en.wikipedia.org/wiki/Christ_the_King_Seminary_(Pakistan)

Zarephath Bible Seminary (ZBS): http://zbspak.org/

FGA Bible Seminary: https://fgabc.org/

Chapter 28   Christians in Crisis and Suffering

Farahnaz Ispahani: *Purifying the Land of the Pure* (HarperCollins, India 2015)

The Jinnah Institute reports: https://jinnah-institute.org/?s=Christians

Human Rights Commission of Pakistan:
https://hrcp-web.org/hrcpweb/annual-reports/

Aasia Noreen:
https://www.worldwatchmonitor.org/the-aasiya-noreen-story/

Bishop John Joseph: https://catholicherald.co.uk/bishop-john-joseph-a-sacrifice-never-to-be-forgotten/

Shahbaz Bhatti:
https://www.catholicnewsagency.com/news/246114/catholics-remember-shahbaz-bhatti-10-years-after-his-assassination-in-pakistan

Earthquake and floods: https://www.christianweek.org/christians-respond-to-catastrophic-pakistan-floods/

Chapter 29   God's Amazing Love for Pakistan

The Pope in Karachi:
https://www.youtube.com/watch?v=QUXfIUgtSuc

Anwar Fazl: https://www.youtube.com/watch?v=_8VEXCknj_k

Karachi's cross: https://www.dawn.com/news/1183333

Chapter 30   The Future for Pakistan's Christians

Informal education: https://weeklycuttingedge.com/informal-schools-also-a-remedy/
https://www.barnabasaid.org/gb/news/editorial-the-vital-importance-of-christian-schools-in-pakistan/

Survey report *For a Better World*:
https://starfishasia.com/resources/survey-report-for-a-better-world/

Hope for the future: https://starfishasia.com/stories/

All-Party Parliamentary Group
for the Pakistani Minorities

The All-Party Parliamentary Group (APPG) for Pakistani Minorities, is a cross-party group of British parliamentarians, who believe that freedom of religion or belief is a fundamental human right. This cherished right is not only enshrined in international human rights law but is also a constitutional guarantee in Pakistan.

We seek to promote the right to freedom of religion or belief in Pakistan for all Pakistani citizens, and aim to raise awareness of issues of discrimination and persecution against religious minorities.

The APPG serves as a unique platform for the British parliamentarians to deepen their understanding of religious minority concerns in Pakistan, and actively contribute to the promotion of freedom of religion or belief within the country.

Our efforts are aimed at fostering an inclusive and tolerant society by lobbying and raising awareness in the Parliament and the UK Government, organizing parliamentary debates, asking Parliamentary Questions, and convening meetings with the parliamentarians, government departments, and members of public. Through these efforts, the APPG for Pakistani Minorities strives to make a meaningful impact on safeguarding and promoting religious freedom in Pakistan

For further information, please contact the Secretariat:
appgpakistaniminorities@gmail.com /
www.appgforpakminorities.com /

Morris Johns (Admin Secretary)
APPG for Pakistani Minorities

STARFISH ASIA
giving hope to the children of Pakistan

Michael Wakely, who compiled and authored this book, founded Starfish Asia, a UK registered charity (No. 1181649), in 2003. Mike's connection with Pakistan goes back to 1979 when he and his wife lived and worked in charitable service in Lahore for about 10 years.

A Pakistani Christian leader came to him one day and said: "Mike, if you really want to help our community, help us educate our children." Mike had never taught a class in his life, but he trusted those who knew their community and they began to provide support – financial and practical – to run schools, especially for Christian children from low-income families.

Today Starfish Asia, together with local staff in Pakistan, is supporting about 50 schools and providing help for teacher training, scholarships, books and furniture, to ensure a good education to raise the hopes and dreams of Pakistan's Christians.

You may find out more about Starfish Asia from our website: https://starfishasia.com and request a brochure or a brief book about the history of the charity. Request *The Starfish Asia Story*.

Write to: mike@starfishasia.com

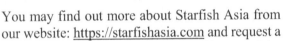
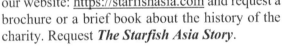

Made in the USA
Monee, IL
30 January 2024